RACING IN
Daytona Beach
SUNSHINE, SAND & SPEED

Robert Redd

THE
History
PRESS

Published by The History Press
Charleston, SC
www.historypress.com

First published 2021

Manufactured in the United States

ISBN 9781467142779

Library of Congress Control Number: 2020944176

CONTENTS

ACKNOWLEDGEMENTS

I would like to thank Arcadia Publishing and Joe Gartrell for their continued support. This is my fourth book with Arcadia, and Joe has been great to work with. The interlibrary loan team at the DeLand Public Library helped me find several sources that were not readily available otherwise. Michael Pinckney, an archivist in the audiovisual department at the National Archives and Ronald Reagan Presidential Library, was very quick to answer questions and to help me track down a much-needed photograph. Jeremy Elliot at the John Hay Center provided me with his research and photographs of a little-known racer. The State Archives of Florida are always easy to work with, and they fulfilled my photograph requests quickly. Peggy Flock generously searched family photographs in order to provide the best copies possible. To everybody else who helped along the way, I thank you.

To my mom and dad, who instilled a work ethic in me through their examples, I will continue to try to "do good work." To my wife, Christina, thank you for your support. I love you.

Now, ladies and gentlemen, start your engines!

INTRODUCTION

There can be little doubt that man likes to go fast. It's all around us. Speed limits have steadily crept up on federal and state roads. Remember the days of the fifty-five-mile-per-hour highway speed limit? Speed is seen in advertising (the Ford Mustang will go from zero to sixty in under four seconds) and entertainment (the world's longest, highest and fastest roller coaster), and movies and television glorify speed, even if it's not on a track. And while these may not be a factor in each of our day-to-day lives, the internet is. Who had dial up internet? Now, 5G is going to be the new standard. Don't get in the way of our social media.

The worldwide fascination with auto racing is living proof of man's need for speed. The appeal of Formula One (F1) around the world cannot be denied. The F1 season is only twenty races long, and yet, in 2017, the series reported that four million spectators attended races; that comes out to an average of two hundred thousand fans per race. This number doesn't even include the massive worldwide television audience. The Indianapolis 500 bills itself as the "Greatest Spectacle in Racing" and regularly attracts a crowd of around 300,000. Local short-track and dirt-track racing events can be found all around the country and regularly have strong attendance, as racers of all ages look to showcase their talents and, with some luck, funding and good equipment to make the leap up the racing ladder.

For many of these local racers, their goal is to hit the bigtime of American motorsports: NASCAR. The three top levels in NASCAR racing are far and away the most popular in the country. More fans flock to NASCAR races than all other series in the United States. That is not to say that there are no attendance concerns; these concerns exist in all live sports—perhaps excluding the NFL. There are myriad things competing for the time and money of consumers, and while attendance at NASCAR races may have gone down over the past couple of years, it is still wildly popular and successful.

The biggest and most popular races are held in Daytona Beach. The Daytona 500 continues to be the biggest draw in the series. To put your name on the Harley J. Earl trophy is a career-defining win. Is it a path to greatness? No. Is it a guaranteed path to career success? No. Are you in elite company that very few can ever claim to be a part of? Absolutely. The July race, which has gone by several monikers in recent years, depending on who is sponsoring the race, may not be as big as the Daytona 500 but is still a race no driver takes lightly. A win at Daytona is to be prized, and now, with recent schedule changes, Daytona International Speedway will have races bookending the "regular season" and will play an even more important role in the "Chase for the Cup."

Bill France Sr. didn't just build Daytona International Speedway out of the blue. For years, the area had been a mecca for speed and racing enthusiasts. From the hardpacked sands of the Ormond Beach area to the beach-and-pavement combination track in Ponce Inlet, racers had flocked to the area for the ideal conditions, the great weather, the scenery and the chance to record their names in the record books of sport.

This book is by no means an attempt to recount all the glorious records, people, monuments, moments and races that are associated with Daytona—that's really too big a proposition for any author to undertake in a single volume. There are some wonderful books that have already been published on specialty topics of the sport. There are several useful and readable volumes that deal specifically with the time trial events held in Ormond Beach. For those interested in the early days of beach racing, I recommend *Beach Racers: Daytona Before NASCAR*, written by Dick Punnett. Mr. Punett has also written *Racing on the Rim*, which also deals with the earliest racing on the beach. Virgil Taylor has written several articles for the Halifax Historical Society journal *Halifax Herald* that cover specific aspects of beach racing. For books on NASCAR, the options are practically endless. For books dealing with racing and Daytona, there are several good ones available; I'd suggest starting with *Daytona Beach: 100 Years of Racing* by Harold Cardwell Sr. This book has dozens of black-and-white photographs that trace the story of racing in the area. Books written by popular drivers are plentiful, as are more general works. To find them, you should stop by your local library or maybe your local independent bookstore. Librarians and bookstore owners are a wealth of knowledge and can help you locate books and materials on whatever aspect of racing interests you.

1
ON THE HARD-PACKED SANDS

On a given day, a given circumstance, you think you have a limit. And you then go for this limit and you touch this limit, and you think, "Okay, this is the limit." And so, you touch this limit, something happens, and you suddenly can go a little bit further. With your mind power, your determination, your instinct, and the experience as well, you can fly very high.
—*Ayrton Senna, three-time Formula 1 world champion*

D aytona Beach can certainly be considered the mecca of motorsports. Daytona International Speedway hosts multiple events throughout the year. Whether you wish to see NASCAR, motorcycles, endurance racing or give the Richard Petty Driving Experience a go, there is something for you. But it's important to remember that racing in Daytona didn't start when the speedway was constructed in the late 1950s; there has been local racing since the early 1900s. Drivers attracted to the hard-packed sands tested their skills and cars as they looked to break land speed records. Later, drivers tested each other in races held on both sand and pavement. And while racing on the beach is a long-ago memory, it is important to give a tip of the hat to those who led the way to Daytona becoming a "bucket list" item for racing fans.

March 26, 1903, is a day of huge importance for racing fans. It was then that the first racing events took place on the sands just south of what is now the Granada Avenue beach entrance. This was a one-mile-long course set up in an attempt to set either world or American land speed records. There were various classes and weights of automobiles awaiting their turn at glory. First up that day was Alexander Winton driving the Bullet #1. He was trying to break the American mile record of just under fifty-two seconds, and if all went well, the forty-six-second world record. In two runs, Winton was only able to clock fifty-six seconds at best. While it didn't set a record, the Bullet #1 is still considered an important move forward in racing, and the car is now in the collection of the Smithsonian Institution. Next up was the Pirate, a car in the under-one-thousand-pound class that was owned by auto manufacturer Ransom E. Olds. Olds and his engineer and driver, Horace T. Thomas were looking to break the time record of just over one minute and thirty-five seconds. With a blazing speed of fifty-four miles per hour, Thomas completed the mile in one minute and six seconds.

There were further trial runs that day, including a new American record set by Oscar Hedstrom on the three-and-a-half-horse-power motorcycle. Two American records had fallen in a single day. The beach was well on its way to becoming the preferred time trial destination. The following day, cars were lined up facing north in order to take advantage of a slight tailwind. Being unfamiliar with the shifting winds, the racers were dismayed to find that the tailwinds quickly became headwinds and worked against their efforts. No records were set that day.

March 28 marked the third and final day of the event. Drivers were again directed southward. While Hedstrom was able to better the world record on his motorcycle, Thomas and the Pirate did not improve either the American or World record mile time. It has been reported that Winton made at least eight attempts in the Bullet #1 but failed to crack the American mile record. In what might be called consolation, both Thomas and Winton were able to better the American kilometer record in their class. An exciting race for fans was also held on March 28; it featured what might be called a drag race between Winton and Thomas. With the Hotel Ormond Challenge Cup at stake, the men raced a mile from a standing start. The lighter Pirate, with Thomas at the wheel, was granted a fifty-yard head start. He stretched the lead to over one hundred yards before the heavier Bullet #1 caught up. Winton and the Bullet won by less than a second.

January 1904 saw the return of racing at the beach, with many more drivers having heard of the benefits of the raceway. As author Dick Punnett pointed out, the multitude of racecars were a combination of factory cars and those driven by the wealthy, men with the means to own and operate an expensive car. These men were often there to be seen, as they did not have the skill or interest to drive the cars themselves. The meet started

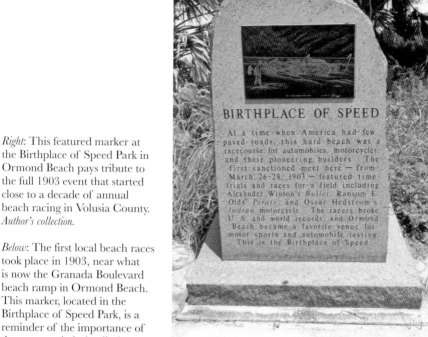

Right: This featured marker at the Birthplace of Speed Park in Ormond Beach pays tribute to the full 1903 event that started close to a decade of annual beach racing in Volusia County. *Author's collection.*

Below: The first local beach races took place in 1903, near what is now the Granada Boulevard beach ramp in Ormond Beach. This marker, located in the Birthplace of Speed Park, is a reminder of the importance of those races. *Author's collection.*

with William K. Vanderbilt Jr. driving his ninety-horsepower Mercedes through the mile-long course in only thirty-nine seconds, setting a new world record. Vanderbilt set records for races in distances of five miles, ten miles and all the way up to fifty miles. He seemingly had little competition that year.

Internal strife started off the 1905 event, with the race to the Ormond starting location now starting in Daytona. And while it was eventually decided to alternate the starting days between the two locations, there were other issues that year as well; temperatures were exceedingly cold, with mornings as low at twenty degrees Fahrenheit, and cars had to be thawed before they could start. Finally, before the meet could officially begin, Frank Croker and his mechanic, Alexander Raoul, were killed in a collision with a motorcycle while practicing.

On January 25, the mile record fell an astonishing four times, with American driver H.L. Bowden completing a run in just under thirty-three seconds or 109.76 miles per hour. Also run in 1905 was the race for the Thomas Dewar Trophy. This featured three heats of four racers. The three winners and the fastest time among the runners-up would compete for the trophy. Louis Ross, driving the "Wogglebug" as it came to be known, featuring two Stanley Steamer engines, took the prize.

The year 1906 was the year of Fred Marriott and the Stanley Steamer. Running for the Dewar Trophy, Fred Marriott made quick work of his competition in the first heat. The Stanley Steamer, with a slow-rolling start as the rules dictated, bested the mile world record by .6 seconds, completing the course in 32.2 seconds. The following day saw Marriott competing in the five-mile race against the temperamental Frenchman Auguste Hemery and his Darracq car and H.W. Fletcher, who was driving a Fiat. The other two drivers false started and did not bother to stop, leaving Marriott to wait for a fair start. On hearing the news, Hemery had none of it and was ultimately disqualified for not agreeing to abide by the judge's ruling. Earlier in the day, a record at this distance had been set, and Marriott had that square in his sights. When he completed his run in just under 2 minutes and 48 seconds, he had another world record. With mechanical issues popping up, the Steamer was only able to finish third in the final heat at the five-mile distance. With repairs made, Marriott returned the following morning and set a mile distance record with a full-speed start. He completed the distance at a speed of over 127 miles per hour.

As the tournament wound down, the final race was the two-mile distance. Nobody had covered the distance in less than one minute. The crowds

Fred Marriott sits in his "Rocket" Stanley Steamer, a car that he would drive to multiple world records in 1906. *Photograph courtesy of the State Archives of Florida, photographer Richard H. Lesesne.*

were lined up, hoping to see that mark broken. Marriott gave it a try but was only able to finish in just under 62 seconds. On his second attempt, he managed to best the elusive mark, completing the course in 59.6 seconds, another record for the Stanley Steamer. This joy was short-lived, as Victor Demogeot later made the run in 58.8 seconds, besting Marriott by almost a full second.

Fred Marriott was to return to Daytona in 1907 with the goal of improving on the one-mile world record at 28.2 seconds set the year before. After several failed attempts, he decided to give it one more try. The races were starting south of the Ormond beach entrance, and while the sands were usually quite smooth, on this date, there were little gullies, or ripples, where the tide had been going out. Marriott was aware of these gullies but insisted on making his attempt. Several eyewitness accounts were recalled by author Dick Punnett in his book *Beach Racers*. Glen Curtis wrote to *Scientific American*, highlighting how the design of the car contributed to the accident. With the lightweight front, the car acted like a glider after hitting the ruts. The back wheels stayed in contact with the sand, only to be destroyed when the front of the car ultimately landed. The car rolled and was torn into

This marker is located in the Birthplace of Speed Park in Ormond Beach and commemorates the successes of Fred Marriott and his famous steam-powered automobile during the 1906 tournament. *Author's collection.*

pieces, with the boiler continuing a short distance past the rest of the debris. Marriott was thrown clear of the wreck and was miraculously not killed. He was hurt, with several lacerations and broken ribs, but he did recover. Using crude timing techniques, it has been estimated that the Steamer was going approximately 150 miles per hour before the crash.

Beach racing continued annually until 1910. In that year, several of the biggest names in the sport converged on Daytona Beach; Barney Oldfield, Ralph DePalma and George Robertson all agreed to attend the March event. Oldfield stole the show on March 23, setting world records in the one-kilometer, two-miles and one-mile stock car divisions. Earlier in the month, he had set a one-mile record, breaking the four-year record that was held by Fred Marriott and his Stanley Steamer. The world record was then held again by a gas-powered car. In the following days, the three-hundred-mile race was rained out and with that came the end of the annual tournament. When the city and sponsors hesitated funding an event for 1911, the City of Jacksonville stepped up and offered the sands of Pablo Beach for an annual tournament.

While the annual tournaments may have ended, the record attempts and racing on the beach did not. In late February 1919, Ralph DePalma returned, this time, driving a Packard. He immediately went about setting a new record on the "measured mile" at just under 150 miles per hour. He later set a record in the mile from a standing start, achieving almost 93 miles per hour. In 1920, the record was broken twice by the same car with different drivers. Tommy Milton eventually held the record at slightly over 156 miles per hour on the mile-long course. In 1922 Sig Haugdahl and his white torpedo-shaped car, the Wisconsin Special, were towed through the beach entrance near the Main Street Pier. It was from there that Sig took several practice runs before making a full-bore effort. When he finished, he became the first driver to reach 180 miles per hour, and while the American Automobile Association did not sanction the speed, it was verified by the rival organization, International Motor Contest Association Inc.

Daytona Beach was silent for several years until in 1927, when Henry Seagrave announced he would be making an attempt to break the 200-mile-per-hour mark in his twin-engine Sunbeam called the Mystery S. The main "mystery" of the car was its two V-12 aircraft engines—one in front and the other behind the driver. Daytona Beach was abuzz on March 29 with the attempt and the return of racing. The course was laid out between the Main Street Pier and the inlet, and the timers were put in place and checked. Nearly all of the city's residents attended, and the fire alarms were sounded to announce the attempt. When Seagrave crossed the line on his return trip, his average speed for the two passes was an incredible 203.98 miles per hour.

Henry Seagrave set multiple land speed records on the sands of Daytona Beach. He was knighted, receiving the title Sir, for his accomplishments. *Photograph courtesy of the State Archives of Florida, photographer Richard H. Lesesne.*

The following year, 1928, saw strong racing talent in Daytona Beach. Major Malcolm Campbell brought his car, the Bluebird, in hopes of regaining the world land speed record. Campbell was to be joined by the young Indianapolis 500 winner Frank Lockhart and his Stutz Blackhawk, along with car owner Jim White and his White Triplex. On February 19, despite poor driving conditions, an impatient Campbell decided to make an attempt. Going against officials' warnings, Campbell made his runs, clocking a new record at 206.98 miles per hour. Frank Lockhart was chomping at the bit to make a run, but his lightweight car could never have handled the rough, weather-beaten course. After waiting three long days, his funds were as short as Campbell's patience, and Lockhart was given the go ahead. He rolled the Blackhawk out for his attempt. Lockhart hit a bad spot on the track, lost control and sent the car into the incoming surf. Luckily, there were alert onlookers who were able to pull the trapped driver from his car. While he was not seriously injured, he had some cuts and bruises, and his season was over. He left vowing to return, however.

In the meantime, car owner Jim White found a driver for the White Triplex, which was so named for the three V-12 engines it contained. As author William Tuthill described it, it was "five thousand cubic inches of noise, smoke, and vibration." Ray Keech, an experienced driver who went on to win the Indianapolis 500, took the wheel. After quite a bit of practice, the time came to show what they had. Officials announced the season would be closing on April 22, and it was on that day that Keech put it all together, running two laps for an average speed of 207.55 miles per hour, enough to take the world record that Malcolm Campbell had set only two months prior.

That same day, now both repaired and healed, Frank Lockhart and the Stutz Blackhawk were ready to make another attempt. Lockhart sped down the course for his first run, and he had his car reviewed and speed calculated in preparation for the return race. As Lockhart valued haste, it is possible the tires were not inspected properly, and they were certainly not changed. On the second pass, a rear tire blew, sending the car careening out of control and flipping wildly. The young driver was thrown from the car and killed instantly.

Despite the lasting negative image from the 1928 season, racers returned in 1929 in search of higher speeds and the glory of being a world record holder. Familiar faces were on hand, including Henry Seagrave; this year, he arrived with his new car, the Golden Arrow. Jim White was also back with his White Triplex. White was again in search of a driver. After his previous encounters with the car, driver Ray Keech had passed up the opportunity.

In 1929, Henry Seagrave drove the Golden Arrow to a new land speed record of over 231 miles per hour. *Photograph courtesy of the State Archives of Florida, photographer Richard H. Lesesne.*

After brief testing, Seagrave started his run to the south, near the lighthouse, gaining speed and running through the measured mile at a record pace. His return attempt was just as strong, and Seagrave was able to regain the land speed record on March 11, clocking an unheard of 231.36 miles per hour. It was a speed that would have been unimaginable just a few years prior. His accomplishments saw him knighted by King George V; he was then Sir Henry Seagrave. Seagrave Street in Daytona Beach is named in his honor.

Jim White found his driver in Lee Bible, a local garage owner who had experience driving on local dirt tracks. After several practice runs, he was certified by officials to be able to make a record attempt. On March 13, he loaded into the White Triplex, hoping to bring the record back to owner Jim White. On his first pass, he was well off record speed at less than two hundred miles per hour. On his second pass, Bible ran into shallow surf, and while he was trying to correct his error, he lost control of the car, flipping it multiple times. The wreck ultimately ejected him from the car. Bible was

Local short-track driver Lee Bible was given the chance to drive the White Triplex when driver Ray Keech declined the opportunity. During a time trial, Bible lost control of his car, was ejected during the crash and lost his life. *Image courtesy of the State Archives of Florida.*

declared dead at the scene, as was a camera man who was hit by the car. After witnessing the tragedy, White decided that was enough and quit racing. Henry Seagrave cancelled plans for another attempt and never raced for a land speed record again. He moved on to boat racing, and in a cruel twist of fate, he was killed in a boat racing accident the following year.

Despite a terrible economy and the racing tragedy of the previous year, there were still those who chose to return to Daytona Beach in 1930. Among them was driver Kaye Don, as he had been chosen to pilot the incredible-looking Silver Bullet, a thirty-one-foot-long car that was said to have achieved 250 miles per hour. Despite the hype, the car only reached 190 miles per hour—the design just didn't work.

Malcolm Campbell had not been to Daytona since his record run in 1928; he had been busy. When he returned in 1931, he brought a revitalized Bluebird with him. With over 1,300 horsepower, Campbell easily upped the world record speed, eclipsing the 245-mile-per-hour mark. He was back in 1932, producing yet another record. This time, he roared along the beach at an amazing 253.97 miles per hour; and yet, he promised more. He stated that his goal was to hit the 300-mile-per-hour mark. He certainly gave it an effort, recording new records of 272.108 miles per hour in 1933 and 276.82 miles per hour in 1935.

This marked the end of land speed beach racing in Daytona. A new location—the salt flats of northwest Utah—had been promoted and was thus discovered by racers. There, Malcolm Campbell achieved his goal and broke the three-hundred-mile-per-hour mark in 1935.

In future years, beach racing moved a few miles south of Daytona Beach to the Port Orange area. The Daytona Beach and Road Course became something of a precursor to the NASCAR racing track of today. The track started on A1A, where the Racing's North Turn Restaurant is located today. Drivers would race south, toward the lighthouse, making a turn east, onto the sands of the beach at the Beach Street entrance ramp. They would then speed back north to complete a lap. The lap length was slightly more than four miles in distance.

In the years before 1949, racing often took place several times a year. Unfortunately, it was often disorganized and proved to be a money-loser for the city and promoter Sig Haugdahl, a racer who had participated in beach racing for several years, including an unsanctioned attempt at a land speed record in his car, the Wisconsin Special, in 1922. Bill France Sr., who had participated in and promoted several of the races, along with some of his friends and other owners and drivers, understood the importance

Above: In 1947, Mrs. Robert C. Weeks (her own name remains unknown) admires the sign posted in recognition of the numerous land speed records set on the "Measured Mile." *Photograph courtesy of the State Archives of Florida.*

Opposite: Sig Haugdahl is shown here sitting in his Wisconsin Special race car. In 1922, he became the first driver to exceed 180 miles per hour during an unofficial test on Daytona Beach. *Photograph courtesy of the State Archives of Florida.*

of banding together and creating a strong organization. Meeting in the latter part of 1947 at the local Streamline Hotel, France's organization put forth and discussed ideas, developed rules and made plans for a racing series. Ultimately, the National Association for Stock Car Auto Racing, or NASCAR, was born from these meetings.

The first beach race under NASCAR was held in 1949. The top names in the sport were there to compete with Red Byron, who won the inaugural Strictly Stock Race. Renamed the Grand National Series in 1950, the race was won by Harold Kite; it was his only career victory. Marshall Teague showed his dominance in 1951 and 1952 by winning both Daytona races; 1952 was his last year in the series. A dispute with Bill France Sr. over racing in USAC-sanctioned races led to his being suspended from competing in NASCAR events. What appeared to be the beginning of a reconciliation between France and the popular hometown driver was cut short when Teague was killed in a testing run at the new Daytona Speedway in February 1959.

It was around 1953 that Bill France saw the writing in the sand. He realized that he was going to need a bigger and more modern track to satisfy the growing popularity of racing, and he began making plans for Daytona International Speedway. His dream took a large amount of money and several years to complete. Construction started in 1956, and the track was ready to host its first event in 1959.

In 1958, Paul Goldsmith started on the pole and won the final race on the beach and road course. Goldsmith had a wide-ranging career as a driver; in addition to running 127 races in the NASCAR Cup Series, in which he won 9 races, he also competed in six Indianapolis 500s, scoring a career-high finish of third in 1960. He was also a motorcycle racer and won the 1953 Daytona 200 while riding a Harley Davidson on the beach and road course. After his racing career was over, Paul Goldsmith was inducted into the Motorcycle Hall of Fame in 1999 and the Motorsports Hall of Fame of America in 2008.

The popularity and convenience of the new speedway, along with the rapid development and an increase in tourism along the beach, helped bring an end to beach racing. While there are still occasional exhibitions, which usually coincide with the annual Speed Weeks, the days of seeing cars drive faster than the posted ten-mile-per-hour speed limit are in the past. With beach driving itself being a controversial issue among locals, the idea of races being held on the sands of Volusia County is an unrealistic one.

2
THE BEST OF THE BEST

The only thing I think about is winning…races and the championship. It's like hunting and fishing. You want to catch the most fish or shoot the most ducks with the least shells. You don't want to be standing there with a whole pile of shells on the ground and one duck.
—Dale Earnhardt on being the best

Every driver longs to be the best. Some drivers specialize; they may be better on superspeedways, short tracks or road courses. To be the best, it takes natural skill, timing, luck, patience, a great team and a dogged determination. Some of the best drivers have never won at Daytona. And there are other drivers, like Greg Sacks, Derrike Cope, Trevor Bayne and Michael Waltrip, who have made career names for themselves by unexpectedly winning at Daytona. Some drivers, such as Ned Jarrett, Terry Labonte and Rusty Wallace, did not win a points-paying race at Daytona. Others, like Richard Petty and Dale Earnhardt Sr., seemed to have a lock on victory lane—points or not. Petty won the Daytona 500 a record seven times in addition to three more wins in the four-hundred-mile race and a win in the first qualifying race in 1977. He finished second multiple times and was known for incredible accidents. He was also known for winning the 1979 Daytona 500 that culminated with an epic fight in the infield between drivers Cale Yarborough and Donnie Allison. His 200th career NASCAR victory also came at Daytona.

Dale Earnhardt, or the Intimidator, as he was commonly called, is still considered by many to have been the best restrictor-plate racer of all time.

While he only garnered one Daytona 500 victory, he finished as a close second five times. He also notched two 400-mile victories, six Xfinity Series victories, six IROC race victories, twelve 125-mile qualifying race victories and a record six Clash Race victories. In all, he had thirty-three career wins. Daytona had been very good to Dale Earnhardt. Daytona was also the track that ultimately cost him his life.

RICHARD PETTY

While Richard Petty may have earned the nickname "The King" from his dominating performances throughout his NASCAR career, he may have earned it from his memorable performances at Daytona International Speedway alone. He came to Daytona for the opening of Daytona International Speedway in 1959. An incredible fifty-nine cars started the race, and Richard finished fifty-sixth, having blown an engine on the eighth lap. Petty Enterprises pocketed a check of $100 from this miserable performance. The race was not an entire loss for the team, however, as Richard's father, Lee Petty, took home the inaugural victory and the $19,050 prize to go with it, albeit three days after the race ended, as it took that long for Bill France to make a decision on the winner after a photo finish.

The rest of 1959 improved for young Richard, as he scored six top-five finishes and nine top-ten finishes, and he finished fifteenth in points, winning the Grand National Rookie of the Year Award—not bad for a young man of only twenty-two years of age.

Petty scored his first wins during the 1960 season, taking the checkered flag at Charlotte, Martinsville and Hillsboro. He also finished second an additional six times. From 1960 to 1962, the Daytona 500 was a mixed bag for Petty. Coming off an impressive rookie season, 1960 was full of promise. Richard qualified with a middle-of-the-pack nineteenth, but when the checkered flag flew, he had earned a third-place finish with his father, Lee, in fourth. Richard also led the second-most laps in the race—twenty-nine—just behind the eventual winner, Junior Johnson.

The 1960 season began an incredible streak for Richard Petty that is probably a rare record that will never be matched. In the years between 1960 and 1983, he finished in the top ten in season points every year except for 1965, a year in which he only competed in fourteen of the year's fifty-five races.

Lee Petty, shown here leaning on his 1953 Dodge Coronet V8 racecar, was the winner of the first Daytona 500, which was held in 1959. He, along with his son Richard and grandson Kyle, are the only three-generation race winners in NASCAR's top series. *Photograph courtesy of the State Archives of Florida.*

A crash in the closing laps of the 1961 Daytona 500 qualifying race led to Richard Petty not being in the starting grid of the race for the last time until 1993, when he was no longer an active driver. He did miss the 1965 Daytona 500, as he was one of the several drivers who boycotted the series after NASCAR banned the HEMI engine. In his time away from the oval, Richard went drag racing with mixed success.

The 1962 season was quite a strong one for Petty; he ran fifty-two races, winning eight, and posting thirty-nine top-ten performances. There can be no doubt that Petty was looking to redeem himself after missing the Daytona 500 in 1961. Starting in tenth place, Petty had worked his way to the lead by lap forty-two. He led a total of thirty-two laps in the race, and at the end, he found himself as the only other lead-lap car as Fireball Roberts notched the victory. He was unable to carry that success over into the Firecracker 400. A crash on lap six ended Petty's day, leaving him in thirtieth position.

Richard Petty really began to show his dominance at Daytona from 1964 to 1968. During these years, Petty ran eleven races at Daytona International Speedway. In that span, he did not start lower than third. He started from the pole four times and won two races: the 1964 and 1966 Daytona 500s. He finished in the top ten in seven of the eleven races. The 1964 Daytona 500 race should be particularly noted, as he led 184 out of the 200 laps on his way to victory, while his 1966 victory included a dramatic comeback from being two laps behind the leaders. Petty won his first two championships in 1964 and 1967. The King had been coronated.

Petty had driven Plymouths since 1960, but for the 1969 season, Petty Enterprises went with Ford. Petty had wanted to drive the Dodge Charger model but executives wanted him to drive a Plymouth. He chose instead to drive the Ford Torino. His results at Daytona were solid; he achieved an eighth-place finish at the Daytona 500 and a fifth-place finish at the Firecracker 400. For the season, he had ten wins and thirty-eight top-ten finishes, ultimately taking second in points behind David Pearson. Despite the success, Petty Enterprises went back to Chrysler, driving a Plymouth for the 1970 season.

The 1970s began with Petty at the top of his game. He was regularly winning ten or more races per year and was always a contender for the points championship. The 1970 Daytona 500 was a short day for Petty, however, as a blown engine only 7 laps in left him with a thirty-ninth-place finish. Another blown engine on lap 139 left Petty in eighteenth position in the July race. Petty reversed his fortunes in the 1971 race, where he started fifth and brought home the victory—the first of twenty-one victories he would score that year. With that win, he became the first three-time winner of the race. He also claimed the runner-up position an amazing eight times, including at the Firecracker 400. Another points championship belonged to him, and the future was looking very bright until Chrysler pulled its factory funding from the team. Even then, funding was critical for a team's success. *Would Petty Enterprises continue into the 1970s?*

Opportunity knocks at strange times, and despite being the most successful driver in the series, Richard Petty was looking for funding. This search led to an incredible twenty-eight-year partnership with STP, and one of the most-recognizable paint schemes in racing was born. Petty's first Daytona 500 with STP was completely forgettable, as a bad valve put him behind the wall after only eighty laps. He was left with a twenty-sixth-place finish. He came back strong in the July race, where he drove a Dodge and finished second to David Pearson. Eight wins and another championship showed that STP had made the right decision in picking a sponsorship recipient.

Richard Petty is shown here with the Miss Speedweeks 1971 celebrating his victory in the Daytona 500. This win made him the first driver to win the prestigious race three times. *Photograph courtesy of the State Archives of Florida.*

Following a bad showing at the 1972 Daytona 500, Petty stormed forward in 1973 and 1974 with wins in each year's Daytona 500s and second-place finishes in each year's Firecracker 400s. During the 1973 Daytona 500, Petty was the recipient of good fortune, as the favorite, Buddy Baker, finished in sixth place after being forced to drop out with a blown engine only six laps from the checkered flag. Petty was also able to overcome being a lap down after a cut tire put him out of sequence on pit stops. The year 1974 would also shine on Petty after another cut tire. The race's leader, Donnie Allison, got caught up in the aftermath of another driver's blown engine and cut a tire himself, allowing Petty to retake the lead and streak to the victory—his fifth Daytona 500 win. The 1973 and 1974 Firecracker 400s would find Petty being the runner-up to David Pearson for the second and third time.

Petty wasn't in contention for the 1975 Daytona 500; in fact, he finished a distant seventh, eight laps down. He did, however, play a factor in the race, as he helped Benny Parsons draft into contention. Parsons was eventually able to take the lead when David Pearson and Cale Yarborough made contact, sending Pearson spinning. Results proved much better in July, as the Petty team roared to victory—his first career Firecracker win.

The 1976 Daytona 500 again featured the duo of Richard Petty and David Pearson battling it out for the win. They had dominated the field, leading a combined 77 laps. On lap 200, Petty was leading as the duo came down the backstretch. Pearson pulled off the pass, and Petty attempted to retake the lead. They touched and spun into the infield. Pearson was able to get his car going again and crossed the finish line for the win, with Petty again finishing in second place. The 1976 Firecracker 400 was a true festival. Held on the bicentennial of the founding of the United States, the winner would have a true prize for their career. Petty qualified a solid third and was considered a serious contender. Unfortunately, on lap 127, his engine blew, and he limped to the garage, finishing in twenty-second place. Cale Yarborough held off David Pearson for the win.

Petty's string of good finishes in the Daytona 500 ended in 1977. Running hard all afternoon to stay in contention, his engine blew on lap 111, leading to a disappointing twenty-sixth-place finish. Things turned out much better in the heat of July. After starting in fifth place, Petty led a race-high 95 laps in a dominating performance, only to be interrupted by a two-hour rain delay about halfway through. He finished a commanding eighteen seconds ahead of second-place Darrell Waltrip.

When Richard Petty arrived in Daytona in February 1978, he had a new car with him, a Dodge Magnum. The race started well for the team, with Petty quickly moving from his sixth-place starting spot to the lead. On lap sixty-one, however, he cut a tire, causing a three-car wreck that included David Pearson and Darrell Waltrip. Petty's day was done, and he finished in a miserable thirty-third spot. Returning to Daytona in July provided a better result, as Petty finished in fourth place, with David Pearson winning yet again. As Petty finished in sixth place in points, the year overall was a down one; it was Petty's lowest full-season finish in points since 1961, and for the first time since 1959, he did not reach victory lane. After twenty years in the driver's seat and 185 wins, some were asking what Petty had left in the tank. *Could he return to form at the age of forty-one?*

Not only did Petty return to form in 1979, he did so at the start of the season with a huge win at the Daytona 500. Qualifying in thirteenth place left him in a spot where danger was lurking all around him. An early crash took out David Pearson, one of his fiercest competitors. Coming to the white flag, Petty had no doubt figured that third place would be his best finish. He was more than half a lap behind leaders Donnie Allison and Cale Yarborough. When Cale tried to pass Allison, he was forced down the track and slid back up into Allison, who was in the lead. They touched several times before finally crashing into the outside wall in turn three. This allowed Petty and Darrell Waltrip to speed by, giving the King his sixth Daytona 500 victory.

The aftermath of the race is considered by many to have been a cornerstone moment in NASCAR history. Allison and Yarborough were out of their damaged cars having a heated discussion when Bobby Allison pulled up and joined in. Things became more animated, and Cale and Bobby started brawling, with part of the melee being shown on national television. As Motor Racing Network reporter Dick Berggren later said, "Nobody knew it then, but that was the race that got everything going. It was the first 'water cooler' race, the first time people had stood around water coolers on Monday and talked about seeing a race on TV the day before. It took a while—years, maybe—to realize how important it was."

Needless to say, the racers had different takes on the cause of the crash. Yarborough put it simply: "He crashed me, it's as simple as that. I was going to pass him and win the race, but he turned left and crashed me. So, hell, I crashed him back. If I wasn't going to get back around, he wasn't either." Allison told a different story: "The track was mine until he hit me in the back. He got me loose and sideways, so I came back to get what was mine. He wrecked me. I didn't wreck him." Bill France, ever the promotional opportunist, when asked about potential fines, replied, "Fine them? Hell, boy, I might give them a raise."

A fifth-place finish was the best Petty could manage at the 1979 Firecracker 400, as he finished two laps behind the leaders. The season, however, was a banner one that came down to the last several races. A tight points battle between Petty and Darrell Waltrip was decided at the final race of the year in Ontario, California. Waltrip was in the lead by a meager two points as they came into the finale, and he had to beat Petty to win the cup. Waltrip finished one lap down in eighth position, but King Richard finished in fifth place, winning the championship by a mere eleven points. His seventh and final Winston Cup Championship was won.

Petty was driving Chevys in 1980, and for the superspeedways at Daytona and Talladega, he ran the Oldsmobile label. Despite qualifying well, a bad clutch put Petty out of the Daytona 500 after 157 laps. The short day put Petty in twenty-fifth position. It was the first of nine races that he did not finish that year. A fifth-place finish in the Firecracker 400 made up for the earlier disappointment. Petty finished fourth place in points, despite only winning two races.

The 1981 Daytona 500 was memorable for Richard Petty for several reasons. Bobby Allison was clearly the driver to beat that week, as he had

There is hardly a more iconic image in NASCAR than "43" painted Richard Petty blue and STP red. *Photograph courtesy of the State Archives of Florida, photographer Eric Tournay.*

dominated the preliminary races coming into Sunday. During the Daytona 500, he led 117 laps and was dominating the field until a fuel miscalculation cost him. He ran out of fuel on the track and had to coast around to pit road. Petty's good fortune and no-tire pit strategy led him to a lead that Allison could not make up. Richard Petty won his seventh Daytona 500. With this victory came the largest purse of his career: $90,575. One fact that is sometimes forgotten about that February afternoon is that Kyle Petty, Richard's son, started his first Daytona 500. Kyle's day was cut short when his engine blew on lap 129, leading to a forgettable thirty-second-place finish. While he never approached the success of his father, Kyle went on to win eight cup races in his career.

A six-car crash on lap 105 took Petty out of the 1982 Daytona 500. While a couple of the cars were able to continue, Petty was done and finished in a distant twenty-seventh place. Daytona didn't get any better for the STP team when they returned in July. A four-car crash involving Petty, Tim Richmond, Cale Yarborough and Harry Gant left Petty with a twenty-fifth-place finish, and eleventh in points. He rebounded and finished the year in fifth place overall. The string of bad finishes continued into 1983. Petty started the Daytona 500 near the front in sixth position, but after only 47 laps, a blown engine ended his day. He recorded a thirty-eighth-place finish. Petty was involved in an accident with Bobby Allison and Dick Brooks on lap 80 of the Firecracker 400, leading to another disappointing finish in thirty-third place.

Petty Enterprises had to be feeling down about Daytona heading into 1984. Good finishes at the track, which had once been very good to them, were hard to come by. Richard and Kyle had both been going through a string of bad finishes due mechanical failures, accidents, bad luck—you name it, the STP cars seemed to find it. While Kyle qualified for the fifteenth spot, Richard was only able to reach thirty-fourth on the grid. However, he understood that starting position didn't always matter. In his drive to reach two hundred victories, he took every opportunity and used every bit of experience he had to try and turn the day around. However, it was another bad Sunday for the entire team. Kyle dropped out after only twenty-one laps with a blown engine. Richard looked good early on, working his way to the front and leading for twenty-four laps, but after ninety-two laps, a broken camshaft sent him to the garage with a thirty-first-place finish.

The 1984 Firecracker 400 began with a remote command from President Ronald Reagan, who called in from Air Force One to tell drivers, "Gentlemen, start your engines." Reagan was on his way to Daytona Beach, where he was to be shuttled from the nearby airport to a press box to share in calling the latter stages of the race with the Motor Racing Network and Ned Jarrett. He was also scheduled to meet with the race winner.

On the track, Petty was running a solid race. He and Cale Yarborough were the class of the field, leading a combined 132 out of the race's 160 laps. They were battling it out when on lap 158, when Doug Heveron, a rookie driver who was only making his ninth start in a cup car, wrecked in turn one. Under the rules of the day, the drivers raced back to the yellow flag, which was shown with the white flag. Whoever got there first would win the race, as there was no green-white-checkered rule at the time. Petty won the sprint, and his 200th win was recorded. He couldn't have asked for more; it was a milestone win on July Fourth with the president in attendance.

Instead of heading to Victory Lane to celebrate, Petty was ushered to an upstairs suite to meet with the president. After the regular celebrations were had, the president, along with Petty and other NASCAR dignitaries, attended a special lunch that featured sponsors Pepsi and Kentucky Fried Chicken. Petty crew chief Buddy Parrot recalled meeting the president that day.

Richard Petty celebrates his two hundredth and final career NASCAR victory with President Ronald Reagan and reporter Jim Lampley. *Photograph courtesy of the Ronald Reagan Presidential Library and National Archives.*

Richard Petty's longtime sponsor STP dedicated this bench at the speedway in his honor in 2017. *Author's collection.*

They put us all back in the back, and they had black plastic all over the fence where people couldn't see in, and we had a picnic that afternoon. The Secret Service walks Robert and Carolyn [Yates] *and Judy and I and Mike Curb and his wife in there to meet the president. When they* [introduced] *me to the president, he had a big chicken leg from Kentucky Fried Chicken, and he was getting ready to take a big bite of chicken, and he looked up, and they introduced me. I've told everybody, "I'm the only person in the world that the president laid his chicken down, wiped his hands off and shook my hand." It was a big deal, and I've got a picture. It was a great time.*

Little did anybody realize that this was the last victory of Petty's career. Over the next eight years, he only scored one more top-ten finish at Daytona, a third-place finish in the 1987 Daytona 500. His 1988 Daytona 500 appearance may have been the most memorable of that eight-year run, but it wasn't memorable for the right reasons. On lap 106, Petty was tapped from behind by fifty-year-old Phil Barkdoll, who was competing in his first Daytona 500, and was sent on the ride of his life. His car was sent airborne, flipping an estimated eight times before coming to a rest and being hit by the oncoming Brett Bodine. Others who were also involved in the wreck were A.J. Foyt, Alan Kulwicki and Eddie Bierschwale. Amazingly, Petty was able to walk away from the wreck unhurt. His car, however, was completely destroyed.

Petty's final race at Daytona was the 1992 Pepsi 400. He started in second place behind Sterling Marlin and even led for five laps. Unfortunately, the July heat in Florida was brutal, and the King retired from the race after eighty-four laps due to fatigue. In his last run at the track, which brought him so much joy and heartbreak, he finished in thirty-sixth place.

DALE EARNHARDT

Dale Earnhardt's climb to finally capturing the elusive Daytona 500, the Great American Race, was one of much drama. He came close numerous times before he was finally able to hoist the Harley J. Earl trophy.

Dale Earnhardt arrived in Daytona as a young man with only five Winston Cup races under his belt in July 1978. He put on a very solid performance, finishing three laps down in seventh position and beating many big-name

This image from the 1979 Firecracker 400 shows Dale Earnhardt taking the "one lap to go" white flag as Neil Bonnett receives the checkered flag and the win. *Photograph courtesy of the State Archives of Florida.*

drivers, including his future car owner Richard Childress. In five races that year, he finished no lower than seventeenth position.

Earnhardt returned in 1979 with a fire that was to become his trademark. As a rookie, he started twenty-seven of the year's thirty-one races, won four pole positions, captured his first checkered flag and led more than six hundred laps. He finished seventh in points and captured the Rookie of the Year Award. His record at Daytona that year was an indicator of his later success. He finished fourth in his first qualifying race, eighth in the Daytona 500 and he led for ten laps at the Daytona 500. He was even better in the summer's four-hundred-mile race, where he finished third. His only major setback that year was a crash at Pocono at the end of July; it kept him out of four races with a broken collar bone.

After starting in the tenth spot, Earnhardt drew little attention in the Daytona 500 until lap forty-four, when Ken Squier from CBS television made the call, "Earnhardt, now there's the kid to watch. This kid Earnhardt in the Osterlund #2, the car out of California, the driver from North Carolina, second-generation driver. His father, one of the most famous short-track drivers in American racing history, the well-known Ralph Earnhardt. His kid looks good today." An unscheduled and longer-than-anticipated pit stop put Earnhardt out of contention, as Richard Petty took the win after Donnie Allison and Cale Yarborough tangled both on and off the track. After the race, people knew who Dale Earnhardt was and would never underestimate his chances again.

The Daytona 500s in 1980 and 1981 again proved successful for the young Earnhardt, as he continued building his name and he recorded two top-five runs. By the 1980 Busch Clash, Earnhardt had already become a master of the draft. As he stated to the *Daytona Beach Morning Journal*, "I tried to stay in second or third place the whole race, knowing I'd have a shot at the leader then. Second place was the place to be on the last lap." A clip of Earnhardt that was played during the race broadcast showed that the young racer was wise and confident beyond his years. In the clip, he said, "But running with these guys I run with, Cale and Richard and Donnie and these guys, you race with them, and if you're smart at all, you pick up on what they're doing, and they'll use it against you, and they'll beat you with it. But, they're not gonna beat me with it but a few times, and

I'm gonna be using it against them." Experience didn't beat Earnhardt in 1980, but pit strategy did. Two late stops did him in. He said, "We shouldn't have changed tires on that last stop. I wish we had just gassed and gone." All wasn't lost though, as Earnhardt won five races that year on his way to his first cup championship.

Despite his 1980 success, he failed to win a pole position and, as such, did not compete in the 1981 Busch Clash at Daytona. He took the defeat graciously, however, and helped the CBS broadcast crew. He also used it as a chance to watch his competition and see how the cars handled the track. "I'd like to be in the clash—no doubt about that—but I think I'll learn a lot from sitting up there and watching." A strong run in the 125-lap qualifying race put the young champion in seventh place on the starting grid. Earnhardt ran a steady race and finished in fifth, his third top-ten finish in three Daytona 500 starts. Unfortunately, his return to Daytona in July did not continue the success. Despite starting third in the field, he completed only seventy-one laps before a vibration issue caused him to park his car for the day.

The 1981 season proved to be an eventful one for Earnhardt off the track. His race team was sold to J.D. Stacy midway through the season. Only a few races into the new ownership, the team split with Earnhardt, and his sponsor Wrangler walked away. A young owner and driver by the name of Richard Childress stepped out of his car and put Earnhardt in the seat. This partnership lasted until the end of the season, when Earnhardt and Wrangler moved again, this time to Bud Moore Engineering, which offered them a three-year contract.

The following two years at the Daytona 500 proved to be more difficult, and they brought the high-flying Earnhardt back to the realities of superspeedway racing. Dale started out well in 1982, winning what is now the Xfinity Race, and starting in tenth position at the Daytona 500. Early on in the race, his car ran out of gas, and as a result, the engine burned a piston. He only completed forty-four laps and finished in a disappointing thirty-sixth position in his debut race for Bud Moore. The Firecracker 400 was equally forgettable, as a blown engine after only eighty-nine laps relegated Earnhardt to a disappointing twenty-ninth place finish.

The 1983 season at Daytona started off with a puff of smoke, as a mechanical set up caused a small bit of oil to release from the #15 car's engine during the Busch Clash. Ignoring a black flag, Earnhardt was racing well at the end but got caught up in a last-lap accident, finishing twelfth. While being fined for his actions, Earnhardt later stated, "Yes, I saw the black flag, but because of the sun, I never saw my number flashing on the board, so

While he only won one Daytona 500, there is no driver more associated with the Daytona International Speedway than Dale Earnhardt Sr., or the Intimidator as he was known. *Photograph courtesy of the State Archives of Florida, photographer Eric Tournay.*

I ignored the flag." The Twin 125 race went better, as Earnhardt pulled off a last-lap pass of A.J. Foyt for the victory. The Daytona 500 did not turn out as well. A blown engine only sixty-three laps in relegated Earnhardt to thirty-sixth place. The Firecracker 400 was better, but it was not a tremendous success; Earnhardt finished two laps off the pace in ninth position. The rest of the year was better, however; he finished having won two races and placing in eighth place in points. Despite this solid finish, a series of driver shakeups after the season led to Earnhardt being reunited with team owner Richard Childress for the final year of his contract, forming one of the most dominant pairings in recent motorsports history.

Coming into the 1984 season, Earnhardt's hopes were high but realistic. The team was young but had a lot of talent in the garage and a proven winner behind the wheel. The Twin 125 race didn't go well, with the team only completing twenty-one laps and finishing in a disappointing twenty-seventh place, a finish that was the second-lowest for Earnhardt at the Twin 125. He started in twenty-ninth position on Sunday in the Daytona 500, but a good drive and pit work had the team right at the front behind Darrell Waltrip and Cale Yarborough on the last lap. Slingshot passes gave Cale the win, and Earnhardt finished a close second, the first of five runner-up finishes in his Daytona 500 career. The season could hardly have started better. Earnhardt's eighth-place performance at the 1984 Firecracker 400 was overshadowed by Richard Petty's two hundredth victory and the appearance of President Ronald Reagan. He closed out with two wins and a fourth-place finish in the points.

With a good year just behind them, the team's hopes were up going into the 1985 campaign. They were dashed quickly, however. After a strong third-place showing at the Twin 125 race, the Daytona 500 became a tremendous let down. Only eighty-four laps in, a blown engine ended the day. "I'm 99 percent sure we cracked a head, and that was the engine failure," stated Lou LaRosa, the team's engine builder. The year wasn't a complete washout, however; the team had four wins and an eighth-place finish in the points, despite not completing nine races.

The team was down, feeling they could have been much better. They thought that perhaps 1986 would be their year. Daytona started off with a bang for the #3 team. Wins in the Busch Clash, the Twin 125 and the Saturday Busch Series Race (Xfinity) led to high expectations for the Daytona 500. Earnhardt and Geoff Bodine had the cars to beat on Sunday. The two were leading as they went into the final twenty laps of the race, and Earnhardt was stalking his prey. Again, pit strategy played into the end of the race. On lap 197, Earnhardt ran out of fuel. Bodine was then able to conserve fuel and take the checkered flag, the biggest win of his career. The Wrangler team finished in a disappointing fourteenth place with engine builder Lou La Rosa the angriest. He said, "It's stupidity; we threw the race away." The season turned out to be a monster one for Earnhardt and Childress; they had five wins, started on the pole once, and Earnhardt won his second championship.

The 1987 season didn't start in traditional Earnhardt fashion. In the pre–Daytona 500 races, he had been dominant in prior years. In 1987, he raced to a fifth-place finish in the Clash, a seventh-place finish in his half of the Twin 125 and a twenty-seventh-place finish (thanks to a blown engine) in the Busch (Xfinity) Race. These results were certainly not up to his standard. The Daytona 500 resulted in a rather nondescript fifth place. It was certainly a strong finish, and it gave the team much to build on—and build they did. Eleven wins, five second-place finishes and only five finishes outside of the top ten led to a second consecutive and third overall Winston Cup title for Earnhardt. Things were looking up at Childress Racing.

The year 1988 was one of change for NASCAR, Dale Earnhardt and the Richard Childress Racing Team. This was the first year of the "restrictor plate," a small aluminum plate with four holes drilled through it. The plates are placed between the carburetor and the intake manifold, helping to lessen the air and fuel flow into the combustion chamber. The intended effect is that it lowers horsepower and, thus, speeds. The 1988 pole speed was over sixteen miles per hour slower than the previous year.

Drivers and teams are often associated with long-term sponsors. The easiest way to recognize your favorite driver is by the paint scheme on their car. For nine years, Earnhardt had driven the blue-and-yellow Wrangler. Beginning in the 1988 season, Goodwrench became his team's primary sponsor. "The Man in Black" was born in NASCAR.

A second-place finish in his heat of the Twin 125 qualifiers, along with a win in the Busch Clash, started the 1988 Speedweeks off with a bang for Earnhardt and his Childress team. An uncharacteristic thirty-seventh-place finish in the Goody's 300 couldn't put a damper on his prospects for the Daytona 500 though. The race was highlighted by a one-two finish by father and son duo Bobby and Davey Allison. Earnhardt finished in tenth place, which was certainly a good finish for most drivers but was maybe not up to Earnhardt's expectations. When the series returned to Daytona in July, Earnhardt was sitting a solid second place in the points and was coming off a fourth-place finish in Michigan. He qualified midpack at twentieth position, but he ran a smart race, leading for fifty-three laps and finishing in fourth place.

With the new restrictor plates and other rule changes, understanding aerodynamics was even more important than before. General Motors and Richard Childress hired Bobby Hutchens to help keep the team a leader on the track. The 1989 season began early.

If you do not post the fastest two speeds in qualifying, the Twin 125s are a way to gain a starting spot in the Daytona 500. If you finish well in your qualifying race and start near the front of the pack, you'll hopefully avoid "the big one" early on. Earnhardt was a master of the Twin 125s, and his performance in 1989 was no exception. Starting his heat in the second position, he finished third behind Terry Labonte and Sterling Marlin in his qualifying race, and he lined up in eighth position at the start of the Daytona 500.

A dramatic wreck in practice for the Busch Race put a minor scare into Earnhardt's team, but Earnhardt walked away unhurt. In discussing the wreck afterward, Earnhardt said:

I had a good grip on the steering wheel. I think that's the one thing that hurts drivers here at Daytona. When they go to flipping, they get knocked loose from the steering wheel. And when that happens, they're just like a dishrag in there. I wear my shoulder harness real tight, and I hold on to the steering wheel real tight. It's probably got knuckle prints in it now.

These were prophetic words considering his future at Daytona. When race day came, Earnhardt finished in a strong third position, giving hope for an even stronger result in the Daytona 500.

In his Saturday practice, Earnhardt's engine started misfiring. Even after changing everything possible, the car still had problems on race day. Earnhardt could run in the draft, but alone, the engine would act up. Despite these problems, he was able to coax the car to a third-place finish. While victory eluded him again, the season was off to a great start. He was never below fourth position in the points and finished second to the eventual season champion, Rusty Wallace, falling only twelve points short.

The Richard Childress Team certainly had much to look forward to in 1990. Starting from the pole in his qualifying race, Earnhardt took the checkered flag, beginning an unparalleled streak of ten consecutive wins in this race. He started second in the Busch Race and again took the checkered flag. He was running so well that some competitors figured he had to be cheating. However, his cars passed all their inspections.

Racing is full of heartbreak and elation. Sometimes, it all comes down to being in the right place at the right time. Some would call this luck, but it is sometimes better to have than skill. Racer Derrike Cope had just such luck at the 1990 Daytona 500. Sunday certainly looked to be Dale's day, as he started in the second position behind Ken Schrader. He led for an incredible 155 laps but not the one that mattered.

After a late round of pit stops, Earnhardt found himself in third position behind Cope and Bobby Hillin Jr., who had both stayed out to gain track position. He was easily able to pass both with his new tires but couldn't shake them and the hard-charging Terry Labonte and Bill Elliott. In turn three, the unimaginable happened: one of the new tires blew on his car. In a post-race interview, Earnhardt described it, saying, "We ran over some debris and cut a right rear tire down…just a quarter of a lap away from victory. Wasn't much you could do about it." In a later interview, Cope stated that he and Earnhardt talked the following week, with Dale saying, "It's not the Daytona 499. It's the Daytona 500. You've got to run 'em all." Earnhardt finished in a heartbreaking fifth position.

Returning in July to the scene of perhaps his biggest professional disappointment, Earnhardt picked up where he left off. Starting in the third position, he rocketed to the lead in the first lap. This move may have kept him from being involved in the massive twenty-three-car pile-up that took place on lap two. Several racers who were expected to contend, including pole-sitter Greg Sacks, were taken out. Earnhardt turned in another dominating performance, leading 127 laps on his way to his fifth victory of the season. He finished the year with nine victories and another cup championship.

Coming off a nine-win and fourth championship season, the team couldn't wait to get back to Daytona in February 1991. Earnhardt was his usual strong self, winning the Busch Clash and leading eighteen out of the race's twenty laps. He won his second consecutive Twin 125 qualifying race, and for good measure, he took the victory at the Goody's 300 Busch series race as well, leading a race-high ninety-one laps. All that remained for the sweep was the elusive Daytona 500 on Sunday.

As often happened in Dale Earnhardt's quest to win the Daytona 500, something unusual occurred during the race. Starting on the outside of the front row, he quickly moved to the lead on lap two before suddenly hitting a seagull that had innocently flown into his path. Trying to make the best of the situation, crew chief Kirk Schelmerdine remembered, "I [said I] hoped it wasn't an albatross. They looked at me like, 'What the [expletive] are you talking about?' There weren't a lot of college readers around the racetrack back in those days." No significant damage was done to the car, and Earnhardt continued on. Later in the race, Earnhardt received a black flag, a stop-and-go penalty for a pit road infraction. Pit road rules had been changed that week due to pit crew injuries that had been sustained during prior races. Rarely one to easily fall in line, Earnhardt later had this to say about the changes, "I don't like the tire rule….There's a lot of torn-up racecars today, and I think a lot of that can be blamed on the pit road rules." Contact with Davey Allison on the backstretch during lap 198 ended Earnhardt's chance to catch leader Ernie Irvan. He was able to salvage a fifth-place finish, while Allison ended up much worse; he was not able to continue and finished in fifteenth place. After the race, an unhappy Allison had this to say, "I was driving my line, and I can't believe how lucky he is. He triggered it, and he kept going. Everything he does, he gets out of it and comes out smelling like a rose." These were words that Allison would no doubt have taken back a decade later had he not perished in a helicopter accident during the 1993 season.

The summer race was a bit of a letdown for the team based on their standards. Earnhardt could only qualify for a disappointing twelfth-place starting position, but he did finish in seventh position after leading only eight laps. Most importantly, he continued to hold his lead in the points and went on to win his fifth cup championship.

The 1992 season started in Daytona, as it had for many years. Earnhardt was dominant; he won his Twin 125 qualifier and the International Race of Champions (IROC) showcase event, and he dominated the field in the Busch Series event, leading an incredible 100 laps out of 120. Earnhardt started the Daytona 500 near the front, as had become his tradition. He got caught up in a thirteen-car wreck in lap ninety-two that effectively ended his day. And while he was able to continue, he finished a lap down in ninth place. While it was certainly a position that most teams would be glad to get out of town with, this was the Intimidator—ninth was not acceptable at Daytona. His return to Florida in July started well enough; he was in third place on the starting grid. But it turned into a horrible day. His engine let go on lap seven, and he finished in fortieth position, last place. He also finished last at Talladega later in the year. He finished the year with only one victory and in a dismal twelfth place in the points.

Crew chief Kirk Schelmerdine left the Childress Team after more than a decade, citing fatigue as a primary factor. The daily grind of being a crew chief had finally taken its toll on him and his family. His departure left one of the top jobs in the sport open. Childress Racing had funding, equipment, manufacturer backing and perhaps the top driver in the sport—who wouldn't have jumped at the opportunity? Childress and Earnhardt ultimately tapped Andy Petree for the job, whisking him away from driver Harry Gant. It was tough going for Petree, who walked into a shop full of crew members who had won multiple cup championships. He rememberd, "It was touch and go for the first six weeks or so that I was there. I didn't think I was gonna make it." The team had to get to know and trust each other if it was going to work.

When the team got to Daytona for the start of the 1993 season, Dale was Dale. He took the checkered flag at the Busch Clash, the Twin 125 qualifier and the Busch Series Goody's 300. Starting in fourth position at the Daytona 500, it looked like 1993 was finally going to be the year Earnhardt finished in first place. He led a race-high 107 laps, but when it came down to Dale versus Dale (Earnhardt versus Jarrett), Jarrett came out the winner, with Earnhardt finishing second. The call from the CBS booth was memorable, as Ned Jarrett, Dale's father, was allowed to call the final lap of the race. He gave viewers an insight into what a spotter might be doing, as he practically gave his son direction around the track. Ned later apologized to Earnhardt for not calling the race in a more unbiased way. Earnhardt understood, however, stating, "Don't you ever forget that I'm a daddy too." That year also marked the arrival of a young driver by the name of Jeff Gordon. Earnhardt and Gordon were to be rivals—both loved and hated—for the next eight years.

For race fans, February 1993 at Daytona had to have seemed like a broken record. The #3 team showed up, dominated the preliminary races and then was unable to win the Daytona 500. A second-place finish for Earnhardt was a huge relief to crew chief Andy Petree, however. While he still butted heads with the team's owner, driver and crew members throughout the year, the season could not have been better. They tallied six wins, including the Pespi 400 on the return trip to Daytona, and they never fell below second place in the points battle. Starting with the tenth week of the season, Earnhardt never looked back on his way to a sixth championship. Andy Petree had found his home.

Dale Earnhardt and Neil Bonnett were good friends. Bonnett had suffered life-threatening injuries in a crash at Darlington in 1990 and had slowly been getting back behind the wheel of racecars. (The itch just doesn't leave most drivers.) During the 1993 season, Bonnett did test work for Richard Childress Racing. He actually made the starting lineup for the race at Talladega, but his race was cut short due to another violent crash. Speedweeks 1994 turned tragic for Earnhardt, however, as his good friend Bonnett passed away from the injuries he suffered during a testing run on February 11 in the lead up to pole qualifying. Earnhardt went out the following day and ran a lap just over 190 miles per hour, good enough to start second in the Daytona 500.

Starting in the second position, Earnhardt was certainly the sentimental favorite—if not the betting favorite—to win. Despite an ill-handling car, he finished in seventh place after leading for forty-five laps. First-time cup winner Sterling Marlin took the victory, holding off Ernie Irvan. On the return trip to Florida in July, Earnhardt started the Pepsi 400 from the pole and finished in a strong third place after leading thirty-one laps. Ernie Irvan finished second again, this time behind Jimmie Spencer, a second first-time cup winner at Daytona that year. Spencer led only one lap, but it was the one that mattered. Earnhardt and Andy Petree had found something, however, as they brought the Richard Childress team another Winston Cup Championship, Dale Earnhardt's record-tying seventh.

Dale Earnhardt dedicated his 1995 Busch Clash victory to his departed friend Neil Bonnett. It would turn out to be his last Clash win, though he continued to run well in the short race. After the race, he stated, "This is a result of all the hard work Neil and the others did on the car a year and a half, two years ago. Neil's legacy lives on." An IROC win and another victory in the Twin 125 heat soon followed.

Starting in the second spot at the Daytona 500, the Childress Team again had momentum, although they seemed a little snakebit. After a late pit stop in lap 186 for fresh tires, Dale started in the fourteenth position when the green flag dropped on lap 189. By lap 196, he had passed some of the best in the game, including Dale Jarrett and Mark Martin, and was in second place, tracking down the leader, Sterling Marlin. He just couldn't quite catch Marlin, who raced to victory lane for the second consecutive year. Afterward, the race crew chief Andy Petree said, "We gave it our best show. We weren't going to finish second the way we were before that last stop."

Summer in Daytona was normal for the Childress Team. Earnhardt qualified to start on the pole at the Pepsi 400; he led eleven laps and finished in a strong third place behind Jeff Gordon and Sterling Marlin. The season was another great one for Earnhardt, Childress and Petree. The team won five races and finished second in the points to Jeff Gordon. But after the season, Andy Petree decided to leave the team, buying the team he used to work for from Leo Jackson. Petree's career as an owner never reached the levels of success he had with Richard Childress. In the years between 1996 and 2003, his cars started 322 races, with only six pole positions and two wins. Earnhardt's new crew chief, David Smith, matched that win total in only one year.

Starting a year with a new crew chief is always challenging, but the Childress Team looked strong going into 1996. The Busch Clash, always an Earnhardt favorite, saw him charge from a sixteenth-position starting spot to a third-place finish, winning his seventh consecutive Twin 125 qualifying race. The forty-lap IROC race was no problem either, as he took the checkered flag in Daytona for the fifth time.

Earnhardt started the Daytona 500 on the pole, edging out the returning Ernie Irvan by only .036 seconds. Amazingly, this was his first pole position for the Daytona 500. As in 1993, it was the Dale and Dale show, with Earnhardt and Jarrett racing for the flag and Ned Jarrett on the call in the booth. Ken Schrader waited behind the two veterans, hoping they would touch. Earnhardt looked on the inside and the outside but couldn't get past Jarrett's Ford, and he finished second again. While it was a strong run, Earnhardt made his feelings known about what he perceived to be the advantages given to Ford, "We couldn't do anything. The damn Fords were too strong. [Did] you not see that? He pulled us by himself. We couldn't draft up to him. Did the same thing in the Clash. They need to wake up. They need to open their eyes." By "they" he obviously meant NASCAR officials.

A fourth-place finish was in store for Earnhardt at the Pepsi 400 in July. After starting in a rather pedestrian seventh place, he drove well enough to keep him in the lead in the points battle. For the season, Earnhardt and his new crew chief finished in fourth place, despite four top-ten finishes in the last five races.

Starting in 1997, Dale was on his third crew chief in three years, as Larry McReynolds came over from the Robert Yates Team. A third-place finish in the Busch Clash and another win in the Twin 125 qualifier started a normal Speedweeks for the team. Dale also had a teammate for the first time at Childress, as a new car for Mike Skinner was added. In the two years prior, Skinner had sixteen wins and a championship driving trucks for Childress. Now, it was time to see what he could do in the majors. As with any new professional relationship, there were some growing pains. Dale was used to being in a one-car operation and the center of attention. McReynolds later said of the situation, "It didn't matter who, Dale was not going to be a good teammate. He just didn't want a second team [member]." Dale's mood didn't lighten even after they had tremendous success on the track. When Mike Skinner won the pole starting position, Dale wanted to know why they were running faster. Larry McReynolds tried to explain to him that the cars had different set ups. After finishing third in the Busch Clash, Earnhardt compared the NASCAR racing to Indy Car. "Once you got nose to tail, that's all you could do. You couldn't pull up, pull out, or nothing." Even after winning the Twin 125, Earnhardt was still fired up, saying, "I don't think we could have won it from second."

With a second-row starting spot, Earnhardt's elusive Daytona 500 win certainly seemed possible. Issues on pit road hampered the team throughout the day, costing them positions on almost every stop. What happened next helped cement Earnhardt's already legendary status not just at the track, but in the sport. On lap 188, a second-place Earnhardt was pushed into the outside wall by a train of cars trying to go underneath him. He and Dale Jarrett touched, sending the #3 car back to the wall and on its roof. Ernie Irvan was collected in the melee, and his engine hood flew off and into the grandstand. It appeared that the day was done for Earnhardt, as he climbed into the track ambulance to get checked out. But suddenly, he climbed out of the ambulance and told the track worker to get out of his car. He fired up the mangled Chevrolet and drove it back to pit road to try and continue. Larry McReynolds said, "I stopped and looked back down pit road, and there's the damn #3 car sitting in the pits. I get back down there, and this car is frickin' destroyed." The team got the car out, and Earnhardt completed a few more laps, gaining valuable points. A thirty-first-place finish was where he finally ended up.

The season between Daytona stops was a mixed bag of finishes, ranging from second to twenty-fifth place. Earnhardt qualified well in the summer heat, starting on the outside pole position, next to his new teammate who took his second Daytona pole of the year. Nobody had anything on the John Andretti and the Cale Yarborough teams that July afternoon, however. They led an incredible 113 laps, and Andretti picked up his first career cup victory. Dale finished strong in fourth position, while his pole-sitting teammate, Mike Skinner, was involved in an early wreck and finished in forty-first. While the team finished fifth in the points (teammate Mike Skinner finished a woeful thirtieth) they did not win a race. That marked the first year since 1981 that Earnhardt did not visit Victory Lane. In addition, he was injured at Talladega.

Racing is a sport that athletes can continue long beyond the years in which others normally hang up the tools of their trades. However, at the age of forty-seven, many wondered how many more quality opportunities Earnhardt would have. The team came to Daytona in 1998, and Dale looked like Dale. In the newly named Bud Shootout, he finished in a strong third place. Once again, he won his heat in the Twin 125 qualifiers, leading all fifty laps, and he was firmly in the second row for the start of the Daytona 500.

During practice, the car was running well. On Saturday, however, the team's luck almost ran out. Earnhardt reported problems, and sure enough, a broken rocker arm and bent push rod were causing problems. Without that final test, Sunday would have been a disaster. As Earnhardt came into the pits on lap 175 for tires and gas, Larry McReynolds made the call to only take two tires, despite Dale wanting four new ones. McReynold's felt his track position was too important, and the eight-second pit stop kept them in the lead as the green flag dropped on lap 178. The #3 car stayed in the lead as the jostling for position began behind it. Coming out of turn two, John Andretti and Lake Speed made contact on lap 199. Earnhardt crossed under the yellow-and-white flags knowing that victory was finally in sight. These were the days before the green-white-checkered format, so all Earnhardt had to do was complete a caution lap and the Great American Race was finally be his. In pulling together his thoughts on the win, Earnhardt said:

It was my time. That's all I can say. I've been passed here. I've run out of gas. I've been cut down with a tire. I've done it all. I wrote the book, and this is the last chapter in this book. I'm going to start a new book next year. It's over with. Every which way you can lose it, I've lost it. Now, I've won it, and I don't care how I won it. We won it.

After the high of winning the Daytona 500, the rest of the season was a letdown. Earnhardt and McReynolds relationship deteriorated, and communication between the driver and crew chief tailed away. Qualifying day was always an adventure, and the team was forced to use multiple provisional starts just to be in the field. Finally, car owner Richard Childress had seen enough, and after the Pontiac Excitement 400 in Richmond, he mandated that Earnhardt and Skinner would be swapping crew chiefs. McReynolds moved to the #31 car, and Kevin Hamlin was moved to the #3. Hamlin would be Dale's crew chief for the rest of his career.

With the summer Daytona race moved to October due to fires throughout central Florida, Earnhardt had his best qualifying position since week nine at Talladega, starting in the fifth position. He only finished in tenth but led forty-one laps. The team finished eighth in points, a great year for many drivers but no doubt a disappointment for the Goodwrench Team.

With the monkey off his back, Earnhardt came back to Daytona in 1999, looking to win two Daytona 500s in a row. He came back with a roar, winning the IROC race and his tenth Twin 125 qualifying race in a row, placing him in the fourth position on the starting grid. With the laps winding down, the racing was intense, with the top drivers, including Earnhardt, Jeff Gordon, Rusty Wallace, Mike Skinner and others, jockeying for position. Teammates Earnhardt and Skinner never hooked up to help each other with the draft. After the race, Skinner had this to say: "I don't want to comment about choices that people went with. I probably wouldn't say anything very nice." His crew chief Larry McReynolds echoed his feelings later on, "They wouldn't work with each other. We could've very well run 1–2 that day. Finally, Dale got off on his own deal." Dale saw things differently than the #31 team, "If we could have worked together, we would have, but we didn't have the opportunity. I mean, look at the racecars out there. You don't just move racecars over [and say], 'Excuse me, I'm coming in here,'" These words don't really ring true, as the Intimidator was known to move people out of his way when he wanted to. With the benefit of hindsight, Earnhardt's crew chief agreed with McReynolds as to why the teammates finished second and fourth, "Jeff Gordon won that race because there were two teammates

Sculptor John Laiba crafted this image of Dale Earnhardt Sr. celebrating his 1998 Daytona 500 victory. Note that Earnhardt is standing on his famous #3. *Author's collection.*

who didn't work together. That's the only reason Jeff Gordon won that race. Earnhardt or Skinner should've won that race. Each blamed the other for not winning the race, and, quite honestly, Richard blamed both of them for neither winning the race." And while the #3 team finished in second and took home a $613,000 payday, it was a far cry from the $1,172,000 that Rick Hendrick and his team collected. In fact, Gordon won more money than Earnhardt and Skinner combined that day.

When he got back to Daytona in July 1999, Earnhardt was sitting in seventh place in points, which was good but maybe not up to his standards. A win at the Pepsi 400 could have jump started the second half of Earnhardt's season. Instead, the Dale and Dale show came to town again, and again, Dale Jarrett was victorious. Earnhardt's Childress teammate, Mike Skinner, finished in a strong fourth position. The season never really improved, and Kevin Hamlin recalled a meeting called by Richard Childress that included the two drivers and two crew chiefs. As Hamlin remembered, "Pretty much, when we walked out and shut the door, I was like 'That was a waste of time.'" Things never did really improve, and Earnhardt finished the year in seventh place in points, and Skinner finished in tenth. For many teams, that would be an incredible year, but for Richard Childress Racing, that had to be improved on. Perhaps to the shock of many, Mike Skinner continued to drive for Childress Racing through the middle of the 2001 season.

The excitement of the 2000s was upon NASCAR, and with it came a new Chevrolet Monte Carlo SS. To say the Goodwrench Team did not like the car at the super speedways was an understatement. For the first time in a decade, the #3 was not in Victory Lane after the qualifying race. Instead, it came in a very disappointing eleventh place and, even more amazingly, did not lead a lap. After the race, Earnhardt gave reporters the story that they were looking for, "That's the worst racing I've seen at Daytona in a long, long time. They took NASCAR Winston Cup racing and made it some of the sorriest racing and took the racing out of the drivers' and crews' hands. We can't adjust. We can't make our cars drive like we want. That's just killed the racing at Daytona. That's all I've got to say." A starting twenty-first-place position awaited the team on Sunday.

Despite the fact that he was driving a car that Kevin Hamlin called "terrible," Earnhardt put the team in contention for a win with less than twenty-five laps remaining. However, it turned into a disappointing finish for both Earnhardt and his son, Dale Jr., and they both appeared to have words for each other after the race. Dale Sr. had this to say about his inexperienced son, "He didn't work at all with anybody. He wanted to pass. That's all he wanted to do, so that's why he finished where he did, [in thirteenth]." Dale Jr. told a different version of the story:

> I just couldn't get anybody to help me. I couldn't get anybody to follow me….My dad too. I thought he would be the first one to help me, but he was the last person who wanted to stay behind me. We did more racing than I wanted to. I wanted to stay with him and stay behind him. Everybody got to racing behind me, and it was either pass or be passed.

Earnhardt's nemesis Dale Jarrett took the victory, his third Daytona 500 win.

Qualifying for the Pepsi 400 was only marginally better for Earnhardt than it had been in February. His team started the race from the eighteenth position. He finished in a mediocre eighth place, one position ahead of his erstwhile teammate, Mike Skinner, and he didn't even lead a lap. The team pulled it together for the year, however, winning two races and having twenty-four top-ten finishes. It was a consistent enough year that Earnhardt finished second place in the points, just behind Bobby Labonte, who was driving for Joe Gibbs Racing. Despite some hiccups along the way, it looked like the team was back on track heading into the off season. *Was an eighth championship out of reach? Would the Intimidator be able to overthrow the King?* The 2001 season seemed to offer a great opportunity to win an eighth championship.

A second-place finish in the Bud Shootout and a third-place finish in the Twin 125 certainly led many to believe that Earnhardt would be a serious contender all year. Not only was Earnhardt driving a top-level car, he was also fielding three cars under his own Dale Earnhardt Incorporated Team. His drivers included his son, Dale Jr.; Steve Park; and his longtime friend and competitor Michael Waltrip. Waltrip was the journeyman younger brother of the legendary Darrell Waltrip. Darrell was then retired and in the FOX broadcasting booth, where, through the years, he again became a legend. In fifteen full-time seasons, "Mikey" had yet to win a race and had less than twenty top-ten finishes, but Earnhardt saw something that others didn't.

Three racing deaths during the 2000 season had forced NASCAR, teams, track owners and drivers to assess their focus on safety. *Was everybody doing enough? What more could be done?* Safer barriers at tracks were just being rolled out; head and neck restraints (often referred to as HANS devices) and other restraint devices were becoming more commonplace for drivers.

When the green flag dropped for the 2001 Daytona 500, Bill Elliott, in an unfamiliar Dodge, led the field through the first lap. The race was quite uneventful as it headed into the last eighty miles; forty of the forty-three cars that started were still running. On lap 174, Robby Gordon and Ward Burton, who had led a race-high fifty-three laps, got together, causing a major wreck that gathered top drivers, including Bobby Labonte and Tony Stewart. A seventeen-minute red flag stopped the race for track clean up.

Tight racing ensued once the green flag dropped. As the lead drivers came to the final lap, Michael Waltip, Dale Jr., Dale Sr., Sterling Marlin and Ken Schrader took the white flag. Marlin remembered thinking that third place would be the best he could hope for. "Well, we're probably gonna run third. I can't get to Michael and Dale Jr." Schrader recalled, "I don't remember shit about [the race], but I remember the end. We came off turn two, and I thought, 'We've got a chance to run third,' and then all hell broke loose."

With Earnhardt Sr., Marlin and Schrader running three-wide, another group of cars was able to catch them. Marlin recalled, "Rusty got pretty close to Dale. That looked like it got Dale loose. Dale kinda came down, crowded me down, got into me. The whole thing started from there." Schrader remembered the scene, "I was right there. When he came up, he just took us with him. My front bumper was in the middle of his door when he came up. I'm in the middle of the racetrack, and Rusty and Sterling are inside us. Everybody's just in that pile, you know?"

After making contact with Schrader, the #3 car was pushed up the track and ultimately into the outside retaining wall while travelling an estimated 160 miles per hour. The angle was just short of head-on. The cars slid down the banking and into the infield grass coming out of turn four. Earnhardt was removed from the car and taken immediately to Halifax Medical Center, where he was pronounced dead later that afternoon. The cause of death was listed as blunt force trauma and a basilar skull fracture—he was dead on impact. The announcement was made by NASCAR president Mike Helton: "This is undoubtedly one of the toughest announcements that I've ever personally had to make, but after the accident in turn four at the end of the Daytona 500, we've lost Dale Earnhardt."

Multiple independent researchers later determined that his death was caused by an inadequately restrained head and neck, and they said that NASCAR's claim of a broken seatbelt played no role in the death. The official NASCAR report differed in opinion, stating, "No single factor can be isolated as the cause of Dale Earnhardt's death," (meaning several factors played a role in the injuries that led to his death). NASCAR also said that while the basilar skull fracture did cause Earnhardt's death, it could not be determined if a head and neck restraint system would have saved the life of the most popular driver in the sport.

Earnhardt's death certainly advanced the cause of driver safety. In the wake of the Earnhardt tragedy, new driver harness systems were developed, the installation of safer barriers was sped up, further research was done and mandates into driver head and neck restraint systems were enforced. In addition, safety requirements for crew members and an increased awareness of the safety of fans became a focus for NASCAR and other racing series. If there has been any silver lining to the death of Dale Earnhardt, it has been that no NASCAR driver has perished at Daytona since his death.

3

IT'S NOT JUST A MAN'S WORLD

But the checkered flag has yet to be dropped on the race to end inequality. It is the job of this generation and those that follow to be vocal and active in order to ensure girls and women have equal opportunities to play and compete at all levels of sport.
—Billie Jean King

The words of tennis legend Billie Jean King, written nearly two decades ago, still ring true today. While there are professional opportunities for women in sports in leagues such as the Women's National Basketball Association (WNBA) and the National Women's Soccer League (NWSL), auto racing is still considered a man's sport, with few women drivers participating, let alone finding real success on the track. The demand for success from sponsors puts tremendous stress on team owners. Time is not an asset for drivers on NASCAR teams and results are expected quickly, especially from high-profile teams and drivers. Success at lower levels means little if it does not translate into the top tiers. If a driver does not produce results on the track, they will find themselves without a seat, no matter how brand- and sponsor-friendly they may be.

For women, it can be even more difficult. Not only are they expected to produce results on the track, but they are expected to look and act a certain way. Their moves on and off track are under more scrutiny than those of their male counterparts. Danica Patrick, while a media darling, a strong brand influencer and no doubt the most famous woman driver in IndyCar and NASCAR history, did not produce enough success on the track to keep her spot in one of the top teams in the sport. Danica's mark, however, may be seen in a few years, as young girls follow in her footsteps.

A woman has yet to win a NASCAR race at Daytona, but that is not to say women have not run well. With the race's bumper-car mentality and the ever-present prospect of "the big one" looming, a female driver could easily find herself in the right place at the right time and bring home a massive victory. How many male drivers has this happened to?

In this chapter, we'll take a look at some of the women who have left their mark on racing in Daytona Beach. We'll start by going back to the days of the Daytona Beach Road Course, when the series was known as Strictly Stock and then Grand National.

SARA CHRISTIAN, ETHEL MOBLY AND LOUISE SMITH

The names of these three pioneer women have been long forgotten—or perhaps never even heard of—by the majority of racing fans today. As the Chinese philosopher Lao Tzu has often been credited with saying, "The journey of a thousand miles begins with one step," and these ladies took the first steps.

Sara Christian was born in 1918 in Paulding County, Georgia. In June 1949, she qualified and started in the thirteenth position at the first NASCAR race held at Charlotte Speedway. However, she gave up her seat to Bob Flock, the brother of a soon-to-be fellow woman driver, partway through the race, and together, they finished in a respectable fourteenth place out of thirty-three cars. In July 1949, Christian raced on the combination dirt and paved track at Daytona, competing against not just men, but her husband, Frank Christian. Frank finished in sixth position, while Sara finished in a promising eighteenth position out of twenty-eight cars, picking up a check for twenty-five dollars for her efforts.

Sara's career was short-lived, and she only competed in a total of seven races over two seasons. She scored a career-high finish of fifth place at Heidelberg Raceway. She had a career-average finishing position of thirteenth place, with a total of $810 in career earnings. In 2004, Sara Christian was added to the Georgia Racing Hall of Fame, an honor she did not get to share in, as she had passed away in 1980.

This page: Ethel Flock Mobley, the sister of racers Tim, Fonty and Bob Flock and the wife of car owner Charlie Mobley, was a racecar driver in an era before seeing a woman behind the wheel was commonplace. *Both photographs are courtesy of Peggy Flock.*

Ethel Flock Mobley was born on March 8, 1914, in Fort Payne, Alabama, a small town in the northwest corner of a state that had a population of less than two thousand at the time. She, along with her brothers, Tim, Fonty and Bob, made up the "Racing Flock Family." Automobile culture was so ingrained in the family that her brother Tim told the story that Ethel was named after the fuel their father used in his car, ethanol.

Racing permeated Ethel's life. She married Charles Mobley, who owned the NASCAR modified car her brother Tim drove. Ethel was a regular competitor in the Modified Series, running over one hundred races. Her career in the Strictly Stock Series only lasted for two events, however. After competing in a June 1949 race in Florida and finishing in an impressive eighth place out of fifty-seven cars, Mobley decided to stay in the state and try her hand in Daytona. During the July 10 race, Ethel and her siblings made history. This was the first Strictly Stock race to feature a brother and sister who were competing, and it was also the first race to feature four siblings. This was also the first Stricly Stock race to feature three women drivers. Ethel placed in a strong eleventh place, only failing to beat one of her siblings, Tim, who finished second. Her prize money was fifty dollars. Later that year, she competed in her second and last Grand National race, finishing in a disappointing forty-fourth place out of forty-five cars at Langley Speedway.

Born July 31, 1916, in Barnesville, Georgia, Louise Smith raced from 1945 to 1956, winning thirty-eight times in various series. In an interview with the *Baltimore Sun*, Smith was quoted as saying, "I was just born to be wild, I tried to be a nurse, a pilot and a beautician and couldn't make it in any of them. But from the moment I hit the racetrack, it was exactly what I wanted." During the 1949 Daytona Beach Race, she finished in twentieth place. Between 1949 and 1952, Smith competed in eleven Grand National Races, accomplishing her highest finish of nineteenth twice.

After her driving career was over, Smith stayed active in the sport. She was known to sponsor drivers and also served as the grand patron of the Miss Southern 500 Pageant for over a decade. Looking back at her life in racing, Smith said, "I enjoyed every minute of it. Didn't make a whole lot of money, but if I could do it again today, I'd do it. And I think I'd make it." In 1999, Louise Smith was elected to the International Motorsports Hall of Fame, the first woman to receive this honor. She passed away at the age of eighty-nine on April 15, 2006. Her headstone, which is shared with her husband, Noah, reads, "First Lady of NASCAR."

And while it may be true that these three ladies are largely forgotten, their accomplishments cannot be overlooked. In an era when most women did

The #91 car, which was driven by Tim Flock of the "Flying Flocks," preparing to leave the dirt portion of the Daytona Beach Road Course. Note the lack of safety precautions for fans shown in the image. *Photograph courtesy of the State Archives of Florida.*

not work outside the home, these trailblazers were forging a path, showing that women could compete on the track when given the opportunity and quality equipment.

JANET GUTHRIE

From humble beginnings, being born in Iowa City, Iowa, on March 7, 1938, Janet Guthrie, through hard work, determination—and perhaps a bit of stubbornness—achieved an unexpected level of success not just in NASCAR, but also in the world of open-wheel racing. She was the first to do many things in racing. She was the first woman to compete in the Indianapolis 500 and the Daytona 500, and she was the first woman to lead a lap in NASCAR's highest level of racing. Her sixth-place finish in the second Bristol race of 1977 still ties her for the highest finish by a woman driver in the Monster Energy Series. In total, Guthrie competed in thirty-three races over a four-year period, notching five top-ten finishes. During her 1977 rookie year, she finished as the top rookie in five of her nineteen starts. Her Champ Car Series career included eleven starts, with one top-five and two top-ten results. Her career-high finish in the Indianapolis 500 occurred in 1978, with a ninth-place result.

Guthrie's NASCAR career was met with skepticism from many drivers, including Richard Petty. In preparation for qualifying for the 1976 World 600, Petty was known to have said, "She's no lady. If she was, she'd be at home. There's a lot of difference in being a lady and being a woman." Her results spoke volumes, however, as she and her underfunded team finished fifteenth, ahead of names such as Bill Elliott, Buddy Baker and Dale Earnhardt. Less than a year and a half later, Petty had different thoughts going into the Daytona 500, "If she had a better ride, she'd probably win one of these [Winston Cup] events."

Janet Guthrie first raced in Daytona at the 1976 Firecracker 400; it was only her second race at NASCARs highest level. Off the trailer, her car was a mess; it was way too loose and close to twenty miles an hour off the lead cars. After driver Cecil Gordon took the car out and reported back the same issues as Guthrie, input changes were made, and Guthrie was able to qualify for the thirty-third position. Although she was still almost eleven miles per hour off the pole speed, she was safely in the field.

July Fourth was a hot, steamy, typical summer day in Florida. The race was fairly uneventful; it only had a single yellow flag in the first 130 laps. On lap 133, Guthrie cut a tire and spun into the infield grass between turns three and four. She was able to coax the car back to pit road, get a new set of tires and finish the race, coming in a highly respectable fifteenth. The Kelly Girl Chevrolet ran three more races with Guthrie at the wheel in 1976, raking up finishes of thirty-third, twenty-second and twentieth places.

The 1977 season opened with the Daytona 500 and its unique qualifying format. With a new crew chief, Guthrie was only able to muster just over 180 miles per hour, which was certainly not enough for the front row but solid enough for a twelfth-place starting spot in the first Twin 125 qualifying race. Guthrie finished eighteenth, not good enough to automatically qualify for the Daytona 500. So, the waiting game began. In the meantime, she and her crew chief, Jim Lindholm, put their heads together, trying to determine what they needed to change in order to make the car more stable so that it could run more quickly. After the second

Twin 125-mile qualifying race, the field was set; Janet Guthrie would be starting in the thirty-ninth position as the first woman to qualify for the Daytona 500.

The issue of her car being too loose had not been settled, however. After serious discussion, major changes were made to the car, allowing Guthrie to increase speeds by more than four miles per hour, and despite scraping the wall during their final practice, the team was ready to make history on Sunday. In spite of going down two laps, the team was posting solid lap times, and Guthrie was in eighth place with only ten laps remaining. It was then that the engine started to let go. She finished the race down two cylinders, bringing the car home in twelfth place, the top finishing rookie and besting many of the biggest names in the sport.

As the heat of summer came on, NASCAR rolled back into Daytona for the sixteenth race of the season, the Firecracker 400. The Kelly Girl Chevrolet had only competed in six races at that point, and Guthrie was in a distant thirty-third place in the points. Qualifying went more smoothly as Guthrie gained experience. She qualified the car midpack, in the twentieth position. This was not ideal but was firmly in the field. The race was hardly as successful, however, as a broken crankshaft only eleven laps into the race ended the day quickly. Richard Petty ultimately won the race, with Guthrie finishing in fortieth position.

Janet Guthrie competed in nineteen out of the thirty races of the 1977 season. She scored four top-ten finishes, led five laps and finished twenty-third in the points. She finished third in the Rookie of the Year battle, just behind Ricky Rudd and Sam Sommers.

Sponsorship money became a problem for Guthrie and her team as they headed into the 1978 season. The team went to Daytona without the funding they needed to compete. During qualifying, Guthrie was unable to crack 180 miles per hour, ending up the twenty-second fastest. A strong finish in her heat of the Twin 125 qualifying races was needed to make the starting grid. Despite starting in tenth position, engine problems only allowed her to finish twenty-eight laps, resulting in a nineteenth-place finish, which ultimately did not allow her to make the Daytona 500.

Things went better for Guthrie as the Firecracker 400 rolled around. While they started far back in the field, in thirty-sixth place, the team kept at it and managed to finish the race in eleventh position, six laps down to the winner. This finish netted the team a prize check of $4,710.

Janet Guthrie raced again at Daytona in 1980. After starting tenth in the second Twin 125 qualifying race, she guided her car to a ninth-place finish

Janet Guthrie was the first woman to compete in the Indianapolis 500 and the Daytona 500, and she was the first woman to lead a lap in cup-level racing in NASCAR. *Photograph courtesy Wikimedia Commons.*

and an eighteenth-place starting position. After finishing the race seven laps down, the Texaco Star Chevrolet with Guthrie at the wheel came in eleventh place. She would only run one more NASCAR race that year, and it was the final in her career. Her final race was the Coca-Cola 500 at Pocono International Raceway in July, where she finished in a disappointing twenty-eighth place after her engine let go after 134 laps.

In the years after her retirement, Janet Guthrie received many honors and accolades for her trailblazing career. In 1980, she was elected to the International Women's Sports Hall of Fame, and in 2006, she was enshrined in the International Motorsports Hall of Fame, and she remains one of only three women who are currently included there. The Sports Car Club Hall of Fame elected Guthrie to their membership in 2018, citing her career success, including winning the 1973 SCCA North Atlantic Road Racing Championship. The Automotive Hall of Fame inducted Guthrie as a part of its 2019 class, citing her wide range of career accomplishments. Visitors to the Smithsonian may view Guthrie's helmet and race suit. Her career was even the focus of an ESPN *30 for 30* piece titled "Qualified." One recognition that continued to elude Guthrie, however, has been the NASCAR Landmark Award, an award given to those who made contributions to the sport. And despite her contributions to the sport, the NASCAR Hall of Fame rules preclude Guthrie from being elected.

There is no doubt that Janet Guthrie left a lasting mark on NASCAR. She proved that women could race at the top level of stock car racing and that they had the ability to be competitive. In talking about the increased opportunities available to women racers today, Guthrie had this to say to ESPN: "As a racer, I wish so badly that I had been given the opportunities that they have now. To race those amazing machines they now have at their disposal. But to think that I may have had a hand in helping them all get to get these chances now—that's humbling. It's truly an honor."

PATTI MOISE

A Florida native, born in Jacksonville, Patti Moise started racing on road courses at the age of sixteen. She made her Busch Series debut at Road Atlanta in 1986; she started in third but finished in thirtieth after her engine let go on the first lap.

The ARCA Series is often home to developing drivers, and Patti Moise was no exception. While she only started five races over three years, two of them were at Daytona, and the other three at the superspeedway at Talladega. In the 1989 and 1990 season openers at Daytona, she won the pole starting position in both races with speeds of 195 miles per hour. In 1989, she finished in nineteenth place after a flat tire took her out with only two laps remaining. In 1990, she crossed the finish line in sixth position.

Moise made three starts at Daytona in the Xfinity Series, and she failed to qualify on five attempts. Her first race occurred in 1988, and she started in twenty-fifth position. A multicar crash on lap eighty-nine relegated the young team to a thirty-third-place finish. Starting in the sixth spot in 1989, Moise's expectations had to be high. An early crash on lap six dashed those hopes, however, and left the team with a thirty-eighth-place finish and a check for barely $2,000. Moise ran her last Xfinity Race at Daytona in 1995. Another poor qualifying run hurt her team. Starting in thirty-fifth position, she was involved in yet another accident before lap ten, leading to a forty-second-place finish. Overall in her career, Moise started 133 races in the series and had four top-ten finishes.

While only she only managed to compile five career starts in what is now the Monster Energy Series, Patti Moise started two July races—but never a

Daytona 500. In 1988, driving for owner Randy Hope, Moise was able to start the Pepsi 400 in thirty-third position. She kept the car out of trouble and finished the race four laps down in twenty-sixth position, beating out drivers like A.J. Foyt, Benny Parsons and Cale Yarborough. Returning to the track in 1989 and driving her own car, Moise again started near the rear of the field in thirty-fifth position. This proved costly. She was involved in a three-car wreck and was not even credited with completing a lap; she finished in the thirty-ninth position. She only competed in one more cup race, finishing in thirty-third place at Talladega after an oil pressure problem took her out.

While her NASCAR career may have not produced the highest level of results, there can be no doubt of her career success. She started an admirable 138 career races in the top levels of the sport.

JENNIFER JO COBB

Born in Kansas City, Missouri, Jennifer Jo Cobb holds the record for most starts in the NASCAR Truck Series by a woman. She has also raced in the Xfinity Series.

Cobb made her Daytona debut in 2010 at the NextEra Energy 250 in the truck series. Starting in the twenty-eighth spot, her day was a short one. In the first lap, a multitruck crash happened in front of her. Cobb's attempts to go low through the infield almost got her through, but she was hit on the passenger side, causing enough damage that she could not return. Memorable for the wrong reasons, her first Daytona appearance netted a thirty-fourth-place finish. She was quoted later as saying, "We've got a long season to go, and I know that we can rebound from this. I still have a lot of faith that we're going to have a great season." She did have a good season, finishing in seventeenth place in the points—the highest finish at the time for a woman in any of the top three tiers of NASCAR.

Cobb also competed in the July Subway Jalapeno 250 Nationwide (Xfinity) Race. Her result there was even more disappointing than her results had been in February. Starting from the forty-first position, it was going to be a long day no matter what. Instead, the day turned short when, on lap eight, her car lost grip, collected the car of Johnny Chapman and ended both of their days. Cobb finished in forty-third position, last place. Trying to remain optimistic, she said, "This is definitely going to take a financial hit for us. This was the only new Nationwide Series car we had in our stable. We have determined that we will be back, but our luck in the Nationwide Series must turn around before long. We are hoping for that turn this Friday at Chicagoland, where we will debut our #13 Ford Fusion." Things did not turn around, and the team did not qualify. They did not run in the series again until it arrived in Kansas, where they finished thirty-fourth.

Cobb's start in Daytona in 2011 started out as a mixed bag. She failed to qualify for the Nationwide Series event. In the truck series, she did make the field, starting way back in thirty-sixth position. As it often happens at Daytona, her starting position was not the end all. Cobb worked her way up and finished the day with a sixth-place finish, a position that still ranks as her career best. Her Nationwide Team returned to Daytona in July hoping for better results. Cobb qualified for the thirty-third starting position but finished in a disappointing thirty-sixth, completing only fifty-six out of one hundred laps. To date, that was her final Xfinity Race at Daytona.

Daytona International Speedway has not been a particularly strong track for Cobb. She did not qualify for the February truck race in the years 2012, 2016, 2017 and 2019. In 2013, she both started and finished in thirty-fifth place after her engine let go. Hoping for better luck in 2014, she again started toward the rear of the field in thirty-fifth position, but she finished the race two laps down in twenty-first. Her Daytona fortunes looked better in 2015, as she picked it up considerably in qualifying, starting in the eleventh spot. The race was a bit of a letdown, however, as she was only able to complete seventy-seven laps, but she did finish in eighteenth position. After not qualifying for two consecutive years, Cobb was back, looking for a good finish in 2018. She qualified near the rear of the field again, and it cost her. A seven-car wreck in lap fifty-six ended the day for Cobb, who was already a lap down at the time. She finished next to last in thirty-first position.

SHAWNA ROBINSON

Iowa-born Shawna Robinson competed in all three of NASCAR's highest levels during her career. She scored a career-high tenth-place finish at the 1994 Zippo at the Glen 200, a Busch Series road race held at the Watkins Glen track.

Robinson experienced some success early on at Daytona International Speedway. Running in the 1988 Charlotte-Daytona Dash Series, she finished in an impressive third place at Daytona. She finished the year third in points and won the Rookie of the Year title and the Most Popular Driver Award. She again finished third in the points the following year.

She made her Busch Grand National (Xfinity) Series debut in February 1991, and she ran her first Daytona race in the series in 1992. It was not a memorable debut. She started thirty-ninth and finished thirty-fourth, completing only sixty-seven laps. It was a rough season, starting only thirteen of thirty-one races and finishing thirty-eighth in points. Not discouraged, she was back for the 1993 season with a new team, Laughlin Racing. They competed in twenty-four of the season's twenty-eight races, including another disappointing finish at Daytona (her engine let go on lap seventy-one, leading to a thirty-second-place finish). The team had little consistency; they did not complete thirteen races and did not finish on the lead lap in any start.

Robinson's next Busch start at Daytona did not come until 2005, when she drove for Keith Coleman. This was again a race of disappointment. Starting in thirty-ninth position, the team did manage to earn a twenty-seventh-place finish and finished on the lead lap.

Shawna Robinson did get the opportunity to drive a Winston Cup car in 2002, when she raced for Beth Morgenthau at BAM Racing. She ran a total of seven races and made the field for both the Daytona 500 and the Pepsi 400, showing she had the ability to run with the best drivers in the sport.

Robinson's 2002 season started with a twenty-fourth-place finish in her heat of the Twin 125 qualifying races, enough to put her in the thirty-seventh starting position for the Daytona 500. She became only the second woman to qualify for the prestigious race. While she came home with a twenty-fourth-place finish, it was not without its pitfalls. She and Bobby Labonte had a close encounter on pit road, and later, she spun into the infield, but she saved the car and was able to continue. She later said, "We accomplished something. It's a step along the way. I want to be competitive. I learned a lot, and I look forward to Talladega." Unfortunately, the team did not qualify at Talladega. She did come back to Daytona in July, however. The results were poor, unfortunately. After starting in twenty-seventh place, she left the race after 110 laps with rear end troubles with her car. She finished in fortieth position in her last start in a cup car.

In 2002, the Iowa Senate passed resolution 212, honoring Shawna Robinson. In part, it read, "BE IT RESOLVED BY THE SENATE, that the Senate recognizes Shawna Robinson for her achievements as a racecar driver, recognizing not only her talent and career accomplishments, but also her determination and encouragement to young women to follow their dreams." In total, Shawna Robinson started seventy-two races in the top three series in NASCAR. Her racing legacy should not be totaled in wins and losses, however. Her legacy as a breast cancer survivor is that of a fighter and a winner—a winner who is one of only three women to ever qualify for the Daytona 500.

JOHANNA LONG

Second-generation driver Johanna Long, who is now married and going by the name Johanna Robbins, began her racing career on tracks around the Gulf Coast of Florida. She had success winning the Gulf Coast Championship and a late-model track championship in Pensacola. She moved up in 2009 and began competing in other racing series, including ARCA. In 2010, she made her Camping World Truck Series debut, finishing in seventeenth position at the AAA Insurance 200. She ran a total of seven truck races in 2010.

In 2011, she ran her first race at Daytona International Speedway, the yearly kick-off NextEra Energy Resources 250. There, she drove for a team owned by her father. She qualified near the top, in fifth position, but a crash on lap seventy-four ended her day early, leading to a thirty-second-place finish.

A move to the Xfinity Series was on the horizon for the 2012 season, and Long made her series debut in Daytona. Her starting and finishing results were mixed, both coming in at twenty-first place. This finish did put her in eleventh place in the points, a solid start to the season. By the time the series made its way back to Daytona in July, however, the team had missed five races and was down to the eighteenth position in points. Daytona proved a good week for the team, as they started in the eleventh position and finished in a solid twelfth, finishing on the lead lap for only the second time of the season. But the prize money and limited sponsorships just weren't enough to keep the team going, and they missed seven more races, a total of twelve in the thirty-three-race season. Between missing races and finishes of thirty-first position or lower in their last three races, the team finished in a disappointing twentieth place in the points for the season.

Johanna Long raced in both the truck and Xfinity series with a career-high finish of eleventh place. *Photograph courtesy of Wikimedia Commons.*

Despite showing promise, the funding needed to run a full slate of races in 2013 did not materialize, and Long and her ForeTravel Motorcoach Team only competed in twenty races. The season opening DRIVE4COPD 300 in Daytona produced a starting grid position of twenty-fifth and a disappointing finish of twenty-seventh after she was involved in "the big one" on lap 115 of 120. Eight cars were taken out of the race. She did, however, beat her fellow woman driver Danica Patrick, who retired on lap thirty-one with a blown engine. This proved to be Long's last race at Daytona, as the team did not compete in the July race.

Johanna Long did not race in NASCAR in 2014, and she only ran one race in 2015. For her career, Long competed in sixty-six races in the Xfinity and Trucks Series. Her career-high finish was an eleventh place at the 2011 WinStar World Casino 400 Truck Race.

In a 2016 interview, Long said:

> *There were so many people that believed in me over the past several years but no one with the money needed to jump-start an effort like you need in NASCAR….When I think about it, I'm just grateful for all the opportunities that I did have in NASCAR. God has given me an awesome life, and hopefully, I can race again soon. There are so many kids that dream of wanting to compete at the highest level of a sport, and I got to do that.*

ERIN CROCKER

Driver Erin Crocker may be remembered more for her relationship with Ray Evernham than she is for her performance on the track. Born in Massachusetts, she began racing quarter midgets at age seven, achieving local success. She later moved on to the World of Outlaws, where she again had success, winning several heat and feature races. Her first taste of the big time came in 2005, when she made six ARCA starts for Ray Evernham

Racing, compiling five top-ten results. Her same-season Busch results, however, were nowhere near as promising, as she only had three starts with no higher a finish than thirty-fifth.

In 2006, she came to Daytona with an ARCA and truck spot with Evernham. Starting the ARCA race from tenth position in the Lucas Oil Chevrolet, she finished on the lead lap in fifteenth position, certainly a respectable run. For the Friday truck race, Crocker started in twenty-fourth position out of thirty-six trucks. She finished the race two laps down in twenty-seventh position. It was an uneventful day, but the truck was all in one piece.

Crocker returned to Daytona, again racing trucks, in 2008; this time, she was driving for David Dollar. After qualifying in the lower half of the field, in the twenty-third position, she kept the pace, keeping the truck clean, and she finished on the lead lap in fourteenth position. She drove again for Dollar the following week in Fontana, California, before being replaced in the driver's seat. That was her final NASCAR race.

Crocker's relationship with owner Ray Evernham came to light and under criticism following a lawsuit from driver Jeremy Mayfield, who claimed the owner was focusing all his efforts on a personal relationship with an unnamed female driver, thus hurting his team. As Crocker was the only female driver in the Evernham stable, it was easy to determine who he was naming. In late 2007, Evernham came clean about the relationship, even suggesting the romance had probably hurt Crocker's career. The couple was married in 2009 and had a baby girl named Cate Susan Evernham in 2015.

TINA GORDON

North Carolina native Tina Gordon had a brief career at the highest levels of NASCAR. She ran a combined thirty races in trucks and the Xfinity Series, with no starts at the cup level. Three of her starts were at Daytona. In addition, she started five ARCA races, with one being at Daytona.

Gordon's first race at Daytona International Speedway was the 2002 ARCA Discount Auto Parts 200. She qualified well, starting the race in the sixth position. When the race was shortened due to rain after only fifty-four laps, Gordon finished on the lead lap in twenty-sixth position.

The 2003 truck race found Gordon starting in the twenty-fourth position out of thirty-six competitors. On lap ninety-nine, while running ten laps down, Gordon was involved in a five-truck crash that ended all their days. She was scored in twenty-second position. Gordon qualified much better for the 2004 truck race, coming to the green flag in the thirteenth spot. Unfortunately, her day was cut short at lap seventy-seven due to suspension problems. She finished the day in the twenty-fourth position.

Gordon started the July 2004 Busch Series Winn Dixie 250 from the next-to-last starting spot, forty-second. She finished the race seven laps down in thirty-second place. That season, her last driving in NASCAR races, produced a fifty-first-place finish in the truck series points after only starting in twelve of the season's thirty-four races.

DANICA PATRICK

There can be little doubt as to who the most famous woman racecar driver of all time is. Without question, it is Danica Patrick. While she is more known for her public relations abilities than for her success on the track, there is little doubt that, when she left the sport, she left a tremendous void that is currently not filled.

She began racing karts as a preteen and eventually worked her way through the open-wheel ranks before landing with Rahal Letterman Racing in 2005. There, she won Rookie of the Year honors after capturing three pole starting positions. In 2008, she earned her only win after outlasting other drivers on fuel mileage. In her IndyCar career, she tallied one win and seven podium finishes in 116 starts.

In 2010 and 2011, she began her move to NASCAR, competing in several Xfinity races. Her first Daytona NASCAR race was the 2010 DRIVE4COPD 300 in January 2010. She qualified well, starting in the fifteenth position, but a twelve-car pileup on lap sixty-nine ended her day, relegating her and her JR Motorsports team to a thirty-fifth-place finish. She returned to Daytona in February 2011, starting fourth and finishing in a respectable fifteenth place, one lap off the leaders. Returning to Daytona in July for the Subway Jalapeño 250, she again showed that she had an ability to run fast and qualify well, starting fourth and finishing tenth for her first top-ten finish of her NASCAR career. Had she not been involved in a last-lap crash, she could have potentially finished even higher.

In 2012, Patrick ran the Nationwide (Xfinity) Series full time for JR Motorsports while she also competed in a handful of cup races for Tommy

Baldwin Racing. She earned the pole position for the February race with an average speed of just under 183 miles per hour. The season started poorly, however, as she and her teammate Cole Whitt came together on lap sixty-one. Patrick's car received considerable damage, and she only completed seventy-two laps, finishing a distant thirty-eighth. After the race, she had this to say,

> *I got a little tap from my teammate, got a little bit sideways, saved it, and then just got hit again and couldn't save it. I don't think it's ever great when teammates come together.* [Cole and I will] *have to figure it out and move on from there. My Go Daddy car was really, really fast. I mean, even when guys were tandem racing right in front of me, I was able to hang right with them. There are so many other days where your car isn't perfect, and nothing happens to you. And you think, "Why, on the days when I have a really fast car, does it have to happen today?" But it did, and we'll move on.*

Whitt replied, "The last thing I want to do is take out a teammate. So, to Danica and her whole crew, I'm sorry. It's just part of this type of racing. I was trying to get hooked up with the #7 car in the tandem draft, and I just made contact getting into the corner, completely my fault."

Using team points from the prior year, the Tommy Baldwin Racing Team was able to assure Patrick a starting spot in the Daytona 500 in 2012. Starting twenty-ninth, Danica was involved in an early accident on lap two; it involved a total of five cars, including superstars Kurt Busch and Jimmie Johnson. She finished in thirty-eighth place. Overall, it had been an exciting and yet disappointing week. Patrick's NASCAR career was really taking off, but the results were not good.

Returning to Daytona in July, Danica found herself sitting in ninth place in the points when the Subway Jalepeno 250 started. Again, she had a good car and made an excellent qualifying run, starting in third position. On lap sixty-six, however, she ended up in yet another multicar wreck that ruined the day. Despite leading the race for thirteen laps, she finished in the thirty-first position, her fourth finish of thirtieth or lower in five Daytona races. The year 2012 was her only full-time year in the series, and despite two tough races at Daytona, she finished an encouraging tenth in points.

Stewart-Haas Racing made a daring move in bringing the lightly experienced Patrick into cup racing full time in 2013, and the team only had her run two Nationwide races during the season. The season started off in Daytona with the Nationwide Series. Patrick had an average qualifying run that allowed her to start in twelfth position, but a blown engine on lap thirty-one ended her day. She finished in a disappointing thirty-sixth place. The cup series was looking up, however, as Patrick put up a speed of over 196 miles per hour during qualifying. It was good enough to put her on the pole, the first woman to earn a pole position in cup racing. With that, she also had the honor of the pole position during the Twin 125-mile qualifying race. There, she ended up shuffled to the back and finished in seventeenth position.

During the Daytona 500, Patrick kept her car out of trouble and led a total of five laps, the first woman to lead a lap at the Daytona 500. She had reached two major milestones in this single race and finished in eighth position. The Go Daddy Team returned to Daytona in July, hoping to build on the success Patrick had had at the Daytona 500. Patrick qualified for the eleventh starting position, almost a full mile per hour slower than pole-sitter Kyle Busch. She ran a solid race, staying on the lead lap, but on the last lap, she was involved in a wreck that took out Kyle Busch, Ryan Newman and several others. She was scored as finishing in fourteenth position. For her rookie season, she finished in twenty-seventh place in the points; the five laps she led during the Daytona 500 were the only laps she led during the season.

Despite her growing pains of being a rookie, Patrick had signs of potential, and after winning the Daytona 500 pole the previous year, it was expected that she would be competitive again. During her Twin 125-mile qualifying race, she finished a in mid-pack thirteenth position and started the Daytona 500 from the twenty-seventh position. She was caught up in a huge wreck on lap 145, which was brought about when Kevin Harvick and Brian Scott came together. Scott then bumped into Aric Almirola, and before all was said and done, thirteen cars were involved. Patrick's day was over, leaving her feeling dejected after a fortieth-place finish. It was not the way she wanted to start the season. Weather played a factor in the July Coke Zero 400. After a poor qualifying run left her in twenty-ninth position on the grid, Patrick pulled it together and finished tenth in the rain-shortened event. The star of the day, however, was Aric Almirola who brought the Richard Petty Motorsports team's #43 car its first win since 1999. The season's results were again disappointing for Patrick, who had hopes and expectations heaped on her. She was only able to finish twenty-eighth in the points.

The Go Daddy Team arrived in Daytona in 2015 hoping to recoup the qualifying magic and perhaps pull off a big victory. After qualifying for the twentieth position in the Daytona 500, Patrick ran a clean race. With no "big one" taking out a large number of drivers, there was plenty of competition at the end of the race; thirty-three drivers finished on the lead lap and only six retired from the race. Danica finished in twenty-first position. Returning to Daytona for the summer race, Patrick and the Stewart-Haas Team were still considered a superspeedway threat, but they only managed a twenty-seventh-place start on the grid. The day was a short one, however, as Patrick, who was already running down a couple of laps, crashed in turn two, ending her day with a thirty-fifth-place finish. She ended the season in twenty-fourth place in the points.

Danica was reaching a critical time in her NASCAR career. She had spent three full seasons in the driver's seat for a top team and didn't have many positive results to show for her efforts. Ultimately, results are what matter to team ownership, and despite having new sponsor dollars from Nature's Bakery, some successful on-track performance was needed. It was hoped that 2016 would be a breakthrough year for Patrick. She finished seventh in her Daytona 500 qualifying race, which led to a sixteenth-place start. With twenty-five laps left in the race, she and Greg Biffle made contact, damaging her car and leading to another disappointing finish in thirty-fifth. Biffle was able to continue on, finishing one position better, thirty-fourth. It was the start of another long season.

Returning to the summer heat of Daytona, Patrick started in the twenty-second spot for the Coke Zero 400. Early in the race, she was tagged with a pit road infraction and had to serve a pit road pass-through penalty. Late in the race, she was involved in "the big one;" a crash that involved twenty-two cars on lap 90. The wreck started when Jamie McMurray and Kyle Larson got together near turn one. McMurray had this to say: "I think somebody got into my left rear, and I don't know if I cut a tire down. After I felt that happen, I just didn't have any control....It's unfortunate. It's part of plate racing." Patrick did manage to get back on the track and complete 130 laps, finishing in twenty-seventh, a credit to her and her crew. With only thirteen top-twenty finishes, Patrick ended the year with a disappointing twenty-fourth-place finish in the points.

Piecing together sponsorship for the 2017 season was difficult, and Patrick had multiple companies serve as her primary sponsor throughout the year. She was in the final year of her contract with Stewart-Haas Racing, and she knew several top drivers would be changing teams at the end of the season. She needed a very strong season to keep her spot on the team. The Daytona 500 did not start her season well. A solid twelfth-place start on the grid gave the team hope. Again, however, Danica ended up involved in the "the big one," a wreck on lap 128 that involved seventeen cars. Patrick's badly damaged car went to the garage, and she finished in thirty-third. By the time the series returned to Daytona, the writing was on the wall. Patrick was twenty-eighth in the points and was running poorly. She qualified well, starting tenth, but again, she was caught up in a major crash. On lap 154, a seven-car pileup triggered by Kyle Larson hitting the outside tri-oval wall ended her day. She finished twenty-fifth and was still a distant twenty-eighth in points.

Heading into the final race of the season at Homestead, Patrick announced what the racing world already suspected. Her regular driving career was over. She addressed reporters, stating, "There was a moment at the beginning of the year where I wondered, 'Is the team just going to shut me down?' Maybe? I don't know. I had to pretty quickly face the music. What if this is the end? It's been running through my head since January." She was not the only driver to leave the sport after 2017; Dale Earnhardt Jr. and Matt Kenseth also announced similar plans but for different reasons.

While Patrick no longer had a NASCAR ride, she did earn a starting spot in the Daytona 500 for a last shot at victory. Starting twenty-eighth, her day was short-lived. She was involved in a seven-car crash just over halfway through the race that left her with a thirty-fifth place finish.

The story of Danica Patrick is not unique to the sport. She was a flashy talent who sponsors loved. She had a bit of success and was pushed along too quickly. It is important to remember that her background was in open-wheel racing, not stock cars. She was not the first open-wheel driver to try to make the switch. Others, like Dario Franchitti, Sam Hornish Jr., Christian Fittipaldi and Juan Pablo Montoya, have made the switch with mixed results at best. Patrick did, however, help further open the door—and ultimately raise the bar—for women in NASCAR. Her accomplishments included being the first woman to win a pole position in the cup series; being the woman with the most starts, most laps led and most top-ten finishes; and she was the first woman to lead laps at both the Daytona 500 and the Indianapolis 500. Her impact on the sport will no doubt be felt in the years to come, as more girls who looked up to her advance through the sport and ultimately better the records she currently owns.

4

YOU CAN'T ESCAPE THE DANGER

The crashes people remember, but drivers remember the near misses.
—Mario Andretti, 1967 Daytona 500 winner

Make no mistake, drivers and their families understand the risks they take every time they go to the track. A large percentage of time, drivers come home safely to their spouses and families. They may be exhausted, but they are complete, able to enjoy the fruits of their dangerous labor. Even drivers involved in accidents almost always walk away. They may be bruised and a bit beat up, but they walk out of the infield care center prepared to get back in the car the following week. Racing is in their blood. They have no other career plans. The lucky ones are those who are able to literally walk away when their career is done. Whether they race their last by choice or are forced to retire because they lack a ride, a retiring driver with their full health is blessed.

However, there are those few drivers who are not so lucky. A slide on the track, a flat tire, fluid on the track, a broken part, driver inexperience and more can have brutal—even fatal—consequences. Racers and fans now often talk of "the big one," the large, multicar pileups that are frequent scenes at high-speed, high-banked tracks, such as Daytona International Speedway and Talladega Superspeedway. For many fans, these wrecks are often the highlights of their weekends. For television networks, these wrecks can be ratings gold that can be mined dozens of times. For drivers, teams and families, however, these symphonies of destruction are nightmares.

Dale Earnhardt Sr. spoke for most racers in 2000 when he said, "I hate restrictor-plate races. All of 'em. None of 'em are good." He said this despite having just won at Talladega for his seventy-sixth NASCAR win. For teams, the very real possibility of a car that costs $250,000 or more going to the scrapyard is a nightmare scenario. And while it is true that different cars are run at different tracks, even well-funded teams cringe at hundreds of man hours and hundreds of thousands of dollars being scrapped as a wrecked car is loaded onto the back of a wrecker. For an underfunded team, "the big one" can be the end of their season. For families, the white-knuckle, edge-of-their-seat competition can be terrifying as their loved ones speed by just inches from other cars in a two-hundred-mile-per-hour dance. *Will their husband or wife, son or daughter, brother or sister be able to put down the window netting and exit the car under their own power?* The answer to this question is never assured.

NASCAR is to be commended for its efforts toward driver safety. With each accident, NASCAR learns more about driver and fan safety. Its efforts in recent years have included improved head and neck restraints; safer cockpits, including improved roll cages and car frames; tire and hood tethers to keep parts attached to the cars during crashes; roof flaps and other aerodynamic improvements to keep cars on the ground after impact; improved fire suit protection; safer barriers on walls; improved fence design for fan safety; and more. NASCAR wants fans to have a good time and enjoy a race, but most of all, it wants to keep these fans, crews and drivers safe and coming back for more.

Safety is an evolving practice, however, and no matter what improvements are made, race teams continue to push the boundaries, and this competitiveness ensures that drivers will be injured. Most will recover to maybe race again. Others, however, will die. From the smallest teams and least-funded drivers to the top-level teams with popular drivers, danger is waiting at every turn, and drivers continue to race head on, challenging themselves and their machines, sometimes to succeed and other times, in rare instances, pay the ultimate price.

In over sixty years of operation, Daytona International Speedway has been a safe track for drivers, despite its dangers of high speeds and high banking. Deaths during races have been tremendously rare. The most notable death that occurred at the track was, of course, that Dale Earnhardt, possibly the most popular driver of all time. Despite being the winner of seventy-six total cup-level races, the track claimed his life on February 18, 2001.

It is only fitting that this book gives tribute to some those brave men who, while they drove with passion, skill and bravery, lost their lives at Daytona in pursuit of their dreams. We'll start on the sands of Daytona Beach.

FRANK CROKER

Born in 1878 as the son of Richard Croker, a famous Tammany Hall politician, Frank Croker was an avid amateur racer, and in January 1905, he was in town testing his Simplex car, the same car he had competed in at the Vanderbilt Cup in Long Island the previous year.

Croker was traveling north with his mechanic Alexander Raoul at an estimated ninety miles per hour. They were rapidly catching a motorcyclist named Newton Stanley, who was on the ocean-side of the car, also traveling north. As the car was rapidly approaching, Stanley suddenly veered left, possibly to avoid an incoming wave. He drove directly into the path of the oncoming racecar. Croker veered sharply left in an attempt to avoid the two-wheeler but still clipped the motorcycle, sheering off a pedal and breaking Stanley's left leg. Both rider and bike ended up in the surf.

During Croker's attempt to avoid the motorcycle, one of his tires flew off the rim, leaving Croker with little to no control. The car flew end over

Frank Croker and his onboard mechanic, Alexander Raoul, were killed after colliding with a motorcyclist during a testing run at Ormond Beach. *Photograph courtesy of the State Archives of Florida, photographer Burr McIntosh.*

end, and Raoul was ejected from his seat. As the car came down, it landed on him, fracturing his skull and killing him instantly. The car continued flipping end over end before rolling sideways. Croker was ejected from the car and was found lying near the wreckage. Croker and Stanley were removed from the scene of the wreck by spectators. Stanley was eventually taken to a hospital in St. Augustine, where his injuries were treated. Croker, who was unconscious when he was found, was taken the short distance to the Hotel Ormond, where it was determined his left leg was broken, his left arm was crushed and two of his ribs had been broken in addition to dozens of bruises and contusions. Raoul's body was left underneath a coat on the beach for more than three hours at the order of the local coroner.

Surgery was performed on Croker to set his arm and leg and to tend to the worst of his cuts. While doctors were initially mildly optimistic, they knew his injuries were quite severe. During the night, Croker lost consciousness and never regained it. He passed away from his injuries early in the morning on January 22, 1905. His distraught mother arrived later that evening.

It was estimated that more than eight thousand spectators were either in attendance or outside the Church of St. Ignatius for the funeral of Frank Croker, though the *New York Times* was quick to add that it believed many were there to support his father, Richard. Frank Croker was buried in an above-ground family crypt in Calvary Cemetery in Woodside, New York.

FRANK LOCKHART

Frank Lockhart was born in April 1903 in Dayton, Ohio. By the age of twenty-three he was racing in the Indianapolis 500, winning the race as a rookie in 1926. He qualified for the pole starting position for the Indianapolis 500 in 1927 but only finished in eighteenth place after mechanical troubles knocked him out of the race.

Lockhart found himself in Daytona in 1928, when he attempted to set a land speed record. While racing in February, he lost control of his car, skidded approximately half a mile and came to rest in the ocean. Spectators rushed to his aid, pulling him from the surf and saving the trapped driver from potentially drowning. As journalist and author Mark Lane said, "Racing has a way of shaking off tragedy fast." Two months later, Lockhart was back on the beach, ready to go again.

Records were falling regularly in 1928. Malcolm Campbell had set a record at nearly 207 miles per hour earlier in the year, only to have it broken by Ray Keech. Lockhart wanted to knock off Keech's 207.55-mile-per-hour record driving the Stutz Blackhawk Special. This silver-and-white car was said to have been "like a projectile" by the local newspaper. The car was aerodynamic and light, so much so that Malcolm Campbell expressed doubts as to its ability to run in the unpredictable sand.

On April 25, 1928, Frank Lockhart made his attempt at the record. On his first run, driving south, he timed in at just over 203 miles per hour. Lockhart's race northward was recorded on film and showed the grisly outcome. Mark Lane described the wreck in a 2018 column in the *Daytona Beach News Journal*, "A rooster tail of sand [can be seen] behind the car just before the rear wheels leave the ground. The car bounces sideways and lands again, almost crashing into a crowd of spectators....The car goes airborne again, then hits the sand, ejecting Lockhart before landing upside down.

This page: Frank Lockhart lost his life in a 1928 accident while driving the Stutz Blackhawk at a speed in excess of two hundred miles per hour. *Both photographs are courtesy of the State Archives of Florida, the photographer for both images was Richard H. Lesesne.*

Lockhart was found 51 feet from the car." The accident was described by fellow driver Wilbur Shaw in his autobiography *Gentlemen, Start Your Engines*, "Halfway through the measured mile, a rear tire blew out. The car veered suddenly to the left into the soft sand. The body of the car tore loose from the frame and somersaulted, end over end, for almost five hundred yards. On the third somersault, it pitched Frank at least seventy-five yards ahead of where the car, itself, finally stopped." No matter the exact detail, Frank Lockhart lay dead on the beach, suffering from a broken neck and back.

Afterward, the cause of the wreck was determined to be a damaged right rear tire. While the cause of the damage is not known for sure, two strong theories emerged. The first was that, during the prior run, Lockhart had locked his brakes and skidded for more than one hundred feet, flat spotting the tire. The second was that he had run over a sharp object or shell on his southern run, and on the return north, the tire blew out. No matter the reason, the damage was not spotted by the crew or driver, and he was cleared for his fateful run north.

Mayor Edward Armstrong ordered flags to be flown at half-staff for two days in honor of Lockhart. Lockhart Street in Daytona Beach was later named in his honor. Even ninety years ago, people tried to philosophically comprehend the dangers of high-speed auto racing. The local newspaper ran an editorial that stated, "He realized the danger, as the public is reading today, yet he drove on into the jaws of death." Lockhart's legend lived on; posthumously, he was inducted into the National Sprint Car Hall of Fame in 1990, and he was later inducted into the Motorsports Hall of Fame of America in 1999. Lockhart's remains were cremated and interred at Columbarium of Faith, Dahlia Terrace, Niche #5938, at Forest Lawn Memorial Park in Glendale, California.

LEE BIBLE

During the late 1920s, speeds were rapidly increasing; owners, drivers and mechanics were becoming more inventive; and speed records were being set on a regular basis. It was a constant challenge to keep up and find drivers who were willing to take the risks needed.

On April 22, 1928, driver Ray Keech set a speed record driving the White Triplex; he topped out at over 207 miles per hour. The White Triplex was a brute of a car, containing three twenty-seven-liter Liberty airplane engines

This page: Lee Bible lost control of the White Triplex on his second record attempt, slamming into a dune. He and photographer Charles Traub were both killed as a result of the accident. *Photograph courtesy of the State Archives of Florida.*

for a mammoth total of 1,500 brake horsepower (bhp). The car had no clutch or gearbox and had to be started with a push start. In early runs, Keech was burned multiple times; the first burn came from a burst radiator hose, and the second came from the exhaust from the front-mounted engine.

Keech's record stood for just under a year before Henry Seagrave shattered it with a record run of over 231 miles per hour. Jim White, the owner of the

White Triplex, vowed to regain the record. He attempted to hire Keech, but he declined due to the dangers of the car. Keech went on to win the 1929 Indianapolis 500, but he perished in a car race only three months after his monumental victory.

White found local garage owner and dirt-track racer Lee Bible and hired him to try to set a new speed record. Despite his inexperience, Bible tested well and was certified by officials to make the attempt. On Wednesday, March 13, 1929, Lee Bible climbed into the White Triplex to try to set a new land speed record. On his first attempt, he only managed about 185 miles per hour. On the trip back north, his speed picked up tremendously but was still well off the record pace at just over 202 miles per hour. Shortly after passing the timing station, the car swerved unexpectedly, and Bible lost control. The local newspaper reported the tragedy, quoting the announcer over the loudspeaker:

> *The Triplex has left the course and rolled over into the dunes. The car swerved and rolled over twice before crashing end over end. Lee Bible was thrown from the wreckage, landing more than twenty feet away; his neck broken. Also killed in the wreck was cameraman Charles Traub, who was struck while trying to get out of the path of the speeding car.*

The accident was so disturbing that all further races were called off for the year. The local newspaper started a relief fund for Bible's widow, and mayor Edward Armstrong again ordered all local flags to be flown at half-staff. The local salvage yard where the car was towed capitalized on the event by charging visitors twenty-five cents to view the destroyed car. Prolific songwriter Andrew "Blind Andy" Jenkins penned the song "Tragedy on Daytona Beach" among his more than eight hundred songs. While Jenkins was often known for his gospel songs, he had a cottage industry of songs based on the darker side of life, including songs about train wrecks, robberies and deaths.

The forty-seven-year-old Lee Bible, who was born in Tennessee, was returned to the state of his birth and buried at Sinking Springs Cemetery in Midway, Tennessee.

MARSHALL TEAGUE

"This speedway (Daytona Beach International Speedway) is safer than U.S. 92," stated mechanic, filling station owner and racecar driver Marshall Teague when he was talking about the newly completed Daytona International Speedway. Two days later, Teague died from the injuries he suffered in a testing crash at that very speedway.

Marshall Teague was a local boy, born in Daytona Beach in 1921; he graduated from Seabreeze High School and spent his life in the racing town. In addition to his racing, Teague owned a full-service filling station in town. Cars were his life. His friend Herschel McGriff described him this way: "One thing about Marshall was he looked like the most unlikely racecar driver you'd ever seen. He had a little pot belly, skinny legs and skinny arms. He looked like the guy watching from the grandstands. Appearances were deceiving." The legendary status of Marshal Teague is tied back to his racing in the "Fabulous Hudson Hornet." It was in this car that Teague competed

Marshall Teague is standing beside his famed Fabulous Hudson Hornet. In 1952, Teague drove the car to victory on the Daytona Beach and Road Course for the second consecutive year in the Strictly Stock Division. *Photograph courtesy of the State Archives of Florida.*

in the NASCAR Grand National Series from 1949 to 1952. He only ran in twenty-three races in that time, but he won an incredible seven of them.

Two of his memorable wins came at the Daytona Beach Road Course, a track that began on Highway A1A in Ponce Inlet (approximately where the Racing's North Turn Restaurant is now located) and headed south, where drivers accessed the beach at the Beach Street approach. They then raced north toward the point where they had originally started, turning west to again access the pavement. The course was approximately 4.2 miles long. The track's combination of dirt and pavement led to some exciting action.

Teague ran the Daytona course a total of four times in the years between 1949 and 1952. In his first Strictly Stock race in 1949, he finished in fourteenth place. The following year, he came in thirty-second after only completing ten of the race's forty-eight laps. But in 1951, Teague began building his legend. Starting in the sixth position, Teague won the race, defeating top racers like Fireball Roberts, the Flock brothers and Buck Baker. He won five of the fifteen races he entered that season, including a dominating performance at Gardena, California, where he led all two hundred laps of the race. He returned to the series in 1952, and while he only ran a total of four races, he won two, including a race at Daytona, leading thirty-six of the race's thirty-seven laps. The 1952 race was shortened by two laps due to incoming tides.

It seemed that NASCAR Grand National racing had its superstar, but Teague also wanted to race events sponsored by USAC and AAA. This caused a rift to form between him and Bill France Sr. and led to Teague being suspended from racing in NASCAR events. This put a big dent in Marshall's plans. He later competed in the 1953 and 1957 Indianapolis 500s. His best finish was a seventh place.

During this time, Bill France Sr. was growing NASCAR and was building what became Daytona International Speedway. The speedway's opening was planned for 1959. France was looking for a driver to set a new world record for closed-course speed. A theory that was put forth said that Teague wanted to get back into NASCAR, especially with the opening of a speedway in his own town. Marshall's daughter Patty Teeters said, "I think he was hoping he could get back in NASCAR since there was gonna be a track in Daytona and he was a local boy." In an interview with Ken Willis Preston Root, the son of car owner Chapman Root, concurred, "That makes sense; I can't say for sure. It was probably a combination of things. It was great publicity for the speedway if it succeeded. It was a way to get Marshall back in the sport without seeming to give in, if you will. Just my opinions."

Teague was hired to drive the Sumar Special Streamliner, an IndyCar. Willis said, "The Sumar Special was fitted with a canopy top, side skirts, and fenders, which could be removed for open-wheel racing. For the Daytona speed record attempt, the Sumar was fully dressed."

On Wednesday, February 11, all was set for the record attempt. Earlier in the week, while he was "just playing around," Teague had run a lap at 171.82 miles per hour. The official attempt should not have been a problem to beat, as the Tony Bettenhausen record was just over 177 miles per hour. His daughter remembered the morning: "I saw him that morning when I got up and went to school. He took me to school a lot, but I don't think he took me that day." Teague arrived at the track in the late morning hours. His first lap was spent working up speed, and he continued that into the second lap. Going into turn one, he bobbled the car, and the left wheels went into the area where the track apron and the banked track meet. Teague quickly lost control of the car, and it became airborne, flipping five times, according to witnesses. The car disintegrated while in the air. Bernard Kahn, the sports editor for the *Daytona Beach News Journal*, stated that the cockpit tore loose from the car and traveled approximately 150 feet, with the deceased Teague still strapped inside. The car itself traveled an estimated five hundred yards from the start of trouble to its final resting spot.

Expert opinion differed as to the cause of the fatal accident. Fellow racer Buck Baker stated, "I always feel that there has to be a reason for a fellow with experience like Teague when he cracks up. Something went wrong with the car, and I can't figure it out." Tom McCahill, the editor for *Mechanix Illustrated*, said, "I don't think it was driver failure. An experienced driver such as Teague would have been able to overcome it if it wasn't for equipment failure somewhere." However, Bill France Sr. stated, "There is no indication of tire or mechanical failure."

Marshall Teague was buried at Daytona Memorial Cemetery, just a short drive from the speedway. He was posthumously elected to the National Motorsports Press Association Hall of Fame in 1966, the National Auto Racing Hall of Fame in 1988 and the American Auto Racing Writers and Broadcasters Association Hall of Fame in 1991.

GEORGE AMICK

"If anything happens, I would like to be buried at Indianapolis." Prophetic words from racer George Amick. Born in Oregon in October 1924, George Amick found himself of age to fight in World War II, and he joined the navy. After the war, he discovered auto racing, where he gravitated toward midget racing. He won sixteen USAC midget feature races.

The realities of racing were never lost on Amick. In 1956, at Vallejo, California, Amick crashed his USAC stock car in the same location as Walt Faulkner, a two-time top-ten finisher in the Indianapolis 500, had crashed just minutes prior. While Amick walked away with only a broken wrist, Faulkner passed away from his injuries. After not qualifying for the 1957 Indianapolis 500, Amick returned in a strong way in 1958, putting his car solidly in the field in the twenty-fifth position. Starting in that position was a positive, as, on the first lap, there was a major accident in turn three. Fifteen racers were involved in the wreck, including Pat O'Connor, a twenty-nine-year-old Indiana native, whose car was violently launched in the air, came down upside down and burst into flames. O'Connor was killed on impact, before the fire even started. Amick finished second, winning Rookie of the Year honors and ultimately finishing second in points to Jimmy Bryan. Amick started forty-three races in his USAC and Champ Car career, winning three times.

While the speeds at Indianapolis and Daytona are often similar, the tracks are quite different; Indianapolis is notoriously flat, while Daytona features high banks. When Daytona International Speedway was completed, Bill France invited USAC to town in an attempt to widen interest in the track. With some trepidation, USAC officials accepted, and a race was scheduled for April 4, 1959. A few of the racers had experience with high-banked tracks, but for most, it was a new experience. They had to quickly learn how to deal with the banking, the high speeds and the uncontrollable winds that wreak havoc on a car and driver. As Tony Benttenhausen said, "Daytona's winds are the trickiest, and it must be driven with great caution."

The week was going well, and Amick won the pole start position for the race with a speed of just under 177 miles per hour. The race was only scheduled for one hundred miles, forty laps. With the new and unknown conditions, it appeared that everyone was going to be safe as Jim Rathmann sped under the checkered flag for the victory. Amick and Bob Christie were fighting for third place in a dash to the finish line. Amick lost control of his car as he headed into the backstretch; the car slid over three hundred feet before striking a guard rail and rolling over several times. Amick was dead at the scene.

"Little George" Amick was buried at Crown Hill Cemetery in Indianapolis. He was posthumously elected to the National Midget Auto Racing Hall of Fame in 2009.

HABE HABERLING

Thirty-three-year-old Harold "Habe" Haberling, a World War II veteran, came to Daytona Beach in February 1961 with dreams of racing in the Sportsman Modified Series, now the Xfinity Series. Haberling was known around his adopted area of Phoenix as a jalopy dirt-track driver. While inexperienced at big tracks, he was no stranger to Daytona. He had run in modified series races in the 1957 beach-road race, and in 1959, he competed in the inaugural modified race at Daytona International Speedway, finishing in a respectable thirteenth place.

On Tuesday, February 21, Haberling was on the track for a practice run but was well off the pace. He was in clear air and didn't have any traffic around him when he lost control of his car. Firefighter Jim White was in the infield and witnessed the wreck. "He lost it as he entered the spiral of the turn. He rolled it both ways, end over end and sideways. I don't know how many times. He didn't hit the high guardrail atop the bank. He went partway up the bank, then came back down to the apron."

The violence of the crash killed the young husband and father of three instantly. His safety belt and shoulder harness were still intact, but his helmet had been torn off. Haberling's body was returned to Arizona and was buried in Greenwood Memory Lawn Cemetery in Phoenix.

DON MACTAVISH

George Cauldwell, a friend of twenty-nine-year-old Don MacTavish, had this to say about the young man: "MacTavish has a feel for a car. Maybe there isn't such a thing as a natural-born racer, but Don is the best damn runner you'll ever see. He loves to go. I'm proud to work with such a guy." A runner Don MacTavish was. Whether it was laying carpet to help finance his first sportsmen car, studying automotive engineering at the Franklin Institute in Boston or running demolition derbies, MacTavish was busy working to improve himself.

His career appeared to be coming along. In 1966, he won the NASCAR National Sportscar Championship, and afterward, he was quoted as saying he wanted to race in the NASCAR Late-Model Grand National Series (now the Monster Energy Cup). "That's what I want most of all." MacTavish was making his way up through the ranks, and in 1969, he was driving in the Permatex 300. Driver Bunky Blackburn was following MacTavish and witnessed much of the accident. Coming off of turn four in the eighth lap, MacTavish slid and started going sideways. Overcorrecting, the #5 Mercury Comet slammed head on into the outside wall at a spot where a metal guardrail covered an opening in the wall. MacTavish hit the end of the wall, shearing off the engine compartment all the way to the firewall. Spinning out of control, he came to a stop facing oncoming racers and was hit by Sam Sommers, a driver out of Savannah, Georgia, who later went on to drive in what is now the Monster Energy Series. Blackburn said, "I've never seen a car disintegrate like that. It went like a bomb. Boy, did that son of a gun come apart. There wasn't much left for Sommers to hit after Mactavish came off that wall."

Sommers was unhurt from the collision, while Blackburn retired due to debris from the wreck damaging his car's oil pan. MacTavish, however, was killed instantly. The violence of the accident left his body crushed and parts of both legs had been torn off. Many observers called it the worst accident they had ever witnessed.

TAB PRINCE

Rookie Talmadge "Tab" Prince came to Daytona in 1970 with the goal of racing the big boys in the Daytona 500. Born in 1938 in the town of Cullman, Alabama, Prince had been racing cars for about a decade before heading to Daytona. He didn't have experience at the Grand National level, as he had only run locally on short tracks.

In January 1970, Tab purchased a Dodge Charger from James Hylton, the 1966 Rookie of the Year. Hylton was switching to Ford for the 1970 season, so he was unloading a surplus car. Being a rookie, Prince's rear bumper was painted yellow, a warning sign to other drivers that they were following an inexperienced driver.

Prince ran well enough to start in the second Twin 125-mile qualifying race. Having just completed the twenty-lap mark, Prince led his car into the steeply banked turn one when his engine blew, sending smoke and oil everywhere. As his car slid sideways, he was hit on the driver's side by the oncoming Bill Seifert, a North Carolina veteran with more than 140 races under his belt. It was estimated that Seifert was traveling around 190 miles per hour at the time of the collision. Johnny Halford, a thirty-nine-year-old driver from South Carolina, could not avoid them and made it a three-car melee. Halford was uninjured, while Seifort suffered cardiac contusions and a cerebral concussion. Despite these injuries, Seifort went on to race thirty-nine times in 1970, finishing eighteenth in points. For Tab Prince, however, the accident proved fatal.

Prince was buried at the Roselawn Garden of Memories cemetery in Decatur, Alabama.

DAVID PEARL

The local Sports Car Club of America hosted a race series known as the Paul Whiteman Trophy, named for the famed band leader who had the nickname the "King of Jazz." The series can trace its local roots to 1957, when races were held at the New Smyrna Beach Airport. That inaugural race was popular, drawing big names like Troy Ruttman, Fireball Roberts and Carroll Shelby. Within a few years, the races were being held on a 3.1-mile road course that incorporated the high banks at the newly opened Daytona International Speedway. Newspaper accounts for the 1970 series of races touted that eleven races would take place over the multi-day event.

Pearl was competing in a July 31 race and was on the second lap of the race when he spun onto the west infield turn section and stalled his car. He came to rest in the center of the track and was hit broadside by Tampa driver Milo Vega. Vega suffered a broken left wrist, a fractured ankle and bruises. Pearl was pronounced dead at the infield hospital as the result of a broken neck and fractured skull.

FRIDAY HASSLER

Raymond Lee Hassler, known to everybody as "Friday," came into his own as a racer in the early 1970s. Still in his midthirties, he was staring to find consistency and was seeing the top ten on a more regular basis. The year 1971 had been his most successful as a racer. Though he only started twenty-nine out of forty-eight races, he finished in the top ten thirteen times and had four top-five finishes. He also started from the pole position twice. He finished the season ranked sixteenth in points, a career high for the nine-year veteran who, at times, had struggled for seat time.

During the 1971 Daytona 500, Hassler finished in a disappointing thirty-sixth place, completing only thirty-eight laps before his engine expired. He came back to Daytona strong in the July race, however, and despite being six laps down, he finished in tenth position. Things were certainly looking up for Hassler's team, a team he owned and often sponsored himself. For the 1972 Daytona 500, he had paired with sponsor "See Rock City in Chattanooga" to start the season off strong.

On Friday, February 17, 1972, Hassler was to compete in the first Twin 125 qualifying race alongside drivers such as Richard Petty, Buddy Baker and Benny Parsons. Less than twenty laps into the race, the "big one" happened. The local newspaper reported that driver Raymond Williams saw the car driven by David Boggs blow a right rear tire. What ensued was a thirteen-car pileup. Driver Verline Eaker ended up in the outside wall, and Hassler slid through the infield grass before slamming into the wall and spinning into traffic. He was then hit by the #54 car driven by Jimmy Crawford before he was driven back into the wall again. Hassler was killed instantly with major skull and neck injuries. His body was returned to Tennessee and was buried at Chattanooga Memorial Park.

DON WILLIAMS

Gordon Lee Williams Jr., or "Don," as he was most commonly known, was the type of racer who dreamed beyond his experience level. Don had been racing for about seven years on local short, dirt tracks when he made plans to race in the 1979 Sportsmen 300, an event that is included in what is now known as the Xfinity Series. It has been reported that, prior to going to Daytona, Williams had never competed on a track that was more than half a mile long. In those days, anybody who could pass a medical exam and pay the license fee could potentially race at Daytona. While those days are long gone, Williams was just one of many who had dreams of the big time and didn't pay their dues along the way.

On a February afternoon, the morning rains cleared, and the crowd was ready for action. The cars were barely warm when, on lap four, Jack Ingram blew an engine going into turn two, leaving a trail of oil and fluids on the track. The cars behind him began to pile up in a fiery ball. Joe Frasson hit the outside wall and then collided with Freddie Smith's car. Frasson's car was then struck by Delma Cowart, igniting Frasson's fuel tank. He sprinted across the infield with burns to his face and eyes. Freddie Smith's car came to a rest in the banked curve and was hit by Don Williams. It appeared that Williams's car had relatively minor damage, including a damaged front fender and a broken out rear window.

To rescuers, it did not appear as serious as it turned out to be. When track workers got to his car, they found Williams unconscious with severe bleeding from his ears and nose. At the hospital, it was determined that Williams had multiple bruises, a broken arm and severe head injuries, including a frontal lobe laceration and a hairline skull fracture. Williams spent three months at Halifax Medical Center in a semi-comatose state before being moved to a facility in Madison, Florida, where he was near family. Later, he was released to his family's care. His health continued to decline, and on March 21, 1989, more than ten years after his crash, he passed away. He was buried at Oak Ridge Cemetery in Madison, Florida.

In the years after the wreck, his family questioned the sequence of events. They claimed NASCAR kept Williams's helmet for many weeks and that they were not told why. A frontal lobe laceration on Williams's head was in a location that should have been protected by the helmet. The family has publicly questioned if the helmet they received from NASCAR was the one worn by Williams in the accident. They have also stated that no representative from NASCAR ever contacted them. The family has also stated that Reverend Hal Marchman, who initially contacted the family regarding the injury, had stated that NASCAR would "take care of everything," including the hospital expenses after the family's $15,000 medical insurance ran out. Marchman emphatically denied making such a statement. The family also had grievances with the France family, who they say never contacted them and also refused to help promote a fund for Don's medical expenses.

Whatever happened in the accident that was ultimately to blame for the long-term injury and ultimate death of Don Williams, there can be no doubt that racing is a high-risk-high-reward sport. It is not always the worst-looking crashes that cause long-term injuries or deaths. Don Williams and his family learned that the hard way.

RICKY KNOTTS

Growing up in the small Michigan town of Paw Paw, a village that was estimated to have a population of less than 3,500, young Benny "Ricky" Knotts began racing cars at the age of fourteen. His father said he raced all over Michigan, Wisconsin, Indiana and down into Missouri. He drove on short tracks and had a bit of success as a member of the American Speed Association, winning races in Toledo, Winchester and Anderson, including the prestigious Redbud 300 in 1979.

Ricky Knotts showed up in Daytona in 1980 having never run in a NASCAR race. He had failed to qualify at Michigan and Charlotte during the previous season. With his father acting as crew chief, the younger Knotts started in the next-to-last position in his Twin 125-mile qualifying race. He was hoping for a miracle to happen. The fifty-lap qualifier had the possibility to propel him into the Daytona 500—and possibly further. Unfortunately, he just wasn't able to keep up with the leaders.

After completing the fourteenth lap, something happened. Knotts drove into the outside retaining wall as he headed into turn one. He spun back down the track, across the exit from pit road and into the grass; this only made him spin further out of control. The car slammed passenger-side-first into an infield retaining wall, destroying the car. Video showed Knotts's head flopping to the left. An inspection of the car showed that the steering column was bent and pushed toward the passenger side of the car. The driver's seat was shifted toward the center of the car. Collected in the crash was fellow rear-of-the-pack starter Blackie Wangerin. Wangerin had driven in NASCAR for twenty years, only qualifying for twenty-seven races, with a career high of fifteenth place. Wangerin came out of the crash with only minor injuries. When questioned later, Wangerin claimed he thought he saw the hood on Knotts's car raise up, leading to the theory that perhaps Knotts's vision was partially blocked.

The race's eventual winner, Donnie Allison, later said, "Something like this always puts a shadow over everything. But when you buckle up in one of those things, you realize what can happen. Race drivers have to accept that."

Allison's brother Bobby, who finished fifth in the other qualifying race, later comforted a reporter who was upset at the happenings and that the activity in the garage kept going. As she recalled the incident, he told her:

> *This is how you pay respect to someone who races. In 1969, my best friend, Don MacTavish, was killed here right before my eyes. He hit the wall and lost the entire front end of his car. The car spun around, and another driver coming out of the turn ran right into him as he sat there, strapped in his seat. It was brutal. But I kept driving. I drove the entire race with tears in my eyes. But I drove because to do anything else would have been giving in to death, and no one on the track or in this garage ever does that.*

Ricky Knotts was buried in Wildey Cemetery, in Paw Paw, Michigan. His headstone features a #31 racecar with the inscription, "Until we meet again, to part no more."

BRUCE JACOBI

"Racing has been my entire life, and it continues to be. Whatever I do hinges around racing. Most every job I ever had has been a steppingstone to the next racetrack," said Bruce Jacobi in a 1980 interview. This is almost a completely true statement. At an early age, Bruce earned money picking corn on land that later became the Salem Speedway in Indiana. In 1965, he was quoted as saying, "I suppose that is what started my interest in racing. I saw my first race there, and I still think it is the greatest track in the world."

When a forty-seven-year-old Bruce Jacobi arrived in Daytona in 1983, he had dreams of racing in his second Daytona 500. He was a veteran of twenty races at the sport's highest level, including a twelfth-place finish in the 1975 Daytona 500. Unfortunately for him, 1975 was his best year, and he had only run five races in the ensuing seven years. Jacobi, who lived near the Indianapolis Motor Speedway, raced in several different circuits in his limited career. In his earlier years, he ran in USAC races, driving midgets, sprint cars and champ cars. He tried multiple times to earn a spot on the grid for the Indianapolis 500 but was never successful, as he had been bumped from the field on multiple occasions.

Danger seemed to follow Jacobi, and during his career, he was involved in several memorable crashes. While racing midgets in 1962 in Champaign,

Illinois, he was involved in a serious crash that almost took his life. Jacobi barrel rolled his car several times and was pronounced dead on the scene. After being transported to the local hospital, it was determined that Jacobi was not dead; rather, he was just in a deep coma. His injuries included a fractured skull, a severe concussion and four different fractures in his right arm. After a lengthy recovery, he came back strong, competing in several open-wheel series during the 1960s. While racing sprint cars on the dirt tracks, he flipped his car on several occasions. During practice runs for the Indianapolis 500 in 1963, he wrecked his car. His NASCAR career was littered with crashes as well, including a violent end-over-end crash during the 1977 World 600. So goes the life of a racecar driver.

Driver Bruce Jacobi hailed from Indiana and raced many types of cars, including midgets, sprint cars and Champ Cars before setting his sights on NASCAR. *Photograph courtesy of Jeremy Elliot.*

Heading into the 1983 Daytona 500, Ya Da Jacobi, Bruce's second wife, said she had never seen her husband happier: "I hadn't seen him that excited in a long time." His racing had been sporadic in the preceding years, and seat time was hard to come by. Only two days before the Twin 125 races, Jacobi was tapped to drive the independent and underfunded #5 Colonial Motors Pontiac.

The Jacobis knew the dangers of high-speed racing. Ms. Jacobi was a veteran of endurance races, having competed in Daytona and Sebring in the 1960s. She said of Bruce, "He said if he had to go, that's where he wanted to go [on a racetrack]." Racing was in his blood. "Bruce said that when he got into a car and buckled in, it was like a part of his body. When he was in the car, nothing else existed."

The conditions were not ideal for the running of the Twin 125 races in February 1983. There had been rain earlier in the morning, and there were strong winds on the track at race time. However, there was nothing to prevent the races from taking place, and Bruce took his spot in the first qualifying race, starting at the rear of the field in the thirty-third position out of thirty-five drivers. On the fifth lap, Jacobi lost control of his car, exiting the second turn while heading into a strong headwind. The car slid down the track, into the swampy infield, and became airborne, flipping end over end before coming to rest near a wall that was protecting drivers from Lake Lloyd. The car was completely destroyed, with only the roll cage still intact. Jacobi suffered severe brain damage as a result of the crash but was in a coma and kept alive with the assistance of a respirator. A month later, he was flown to his home state of Indiana so family could be close by.

Bruce Jacobi spent four years in a coma before passing away from his injuries on February 4, 1987, at the age of fifty-one. He was buried in Crown Hill Cemetery in Salem, Indiana.

FRANCIS AFFLECK

Born in March 1950 in Canada, Francis Affleck hardly seemed the type to pursue racing on the high banks of Daytona. He raced late-model cars in his home country before moving to Charlotte, North Carolina, in 1977, where he continued to race on local tracks.

During the 1984 season, Affleck raced three times in what is now the Xfinity Series, including the season-opening Goody's 300 in Daytona. While he only finished thirty-first, he gained experience. He returned in 1985 with a goal to make the field for the ARCA 200. During a February 7 practice, Affleck lost control of his car at around 180 miles per hour. The car violently flipped multiple times on the backstretch. The window netting on Affleck's car failed, and he was partially ejected from the car. He died instantly from massive head, neck and internal injuries.

JOE YOUNG

Crew member Tom Phelps remembered Daytona Dash series driver Joe Young, saying, "He sure loved racing, but what can you say? This kind of thing happens. Joe knew it could happen to him." Joe Young, a thirty-eight-year-old driver from Richmond, Virginia, was competing in his eighth Komfort Koach 200. On lap thirty-six of the eighty-lap race, driver Karen Schulz, an experienced driver who had been named the Series Rookie of the Year two years prior, lost control of her car as she came out of the backstretch. She recalled, "The tire blew or something broke, and the car let go on me as I was going into turn three. I spun to the infield, and when I hit the flat part, two tires went flat. Then, somebody tapped me, and Lord, I don't know what happened after that."

The pack behind her then split, trying to avoid her, and cars started spinning out of control. One of those, the #5 Chevrolet driven by Joe Young, came to a stop facing the wrong direction on the track. Young's car was hit head on by the oncoming Duell Sturgill, a thirty-three-year-old dentist from Staffordsville, Kentucky, crumpling the car into the cockpit area. Rescue workers told crew members that Young was killed instantly and was dead before they arrived. Volusia County medical examiner Arthur Schwartz stated that Young died from "a fracture at the base of the skull." Sturgill suffered compound fractures to both ankles but lived to race another day.

JULIUS "SLICK" JOHNSON

Running in only his second ARCA race, Julius "Slick" Johnson had high hopes after an initial qualifying run put him in the twelfth position on the starting grid. "Slick" was a veteran driver, having competed in dozens of late-model and Grand National races, and he also participated in sixty-eight races at NASCAR's top level. He was familiar with superspeedway racing, as he had raced at both Talladega and Daytona, including at the 1980 Daytona 500, where he finished in fourteenth place. His most successful season occurred in 1980, when he started eighteen cup-level races and had five top-ten finishes, finishing twenty-third in points. He scored his career-high finish of eighth place twice that year at the Holly Farms 400 and the American 500.

The February 11, 1990 eighty-lap ARCA 200 had been pretty uneventful for Johnson. He was running a lap down on lap seventy-five when he brushed the wall in turn three, causing a major wreck that involved a total of seven cars, including those of Graham Taylor, David Simko, Kevin Gundaker, Chris Gehrke, Billy Thomas and Cecil Eunice. Johnson was hit at least three times, including a final hit directly on the driver's side. David Simko, who was the driver of the first car to hit Johnson's, later said, "The #95 car lost it in three and four, got down on the apron and shot back up the track. There was so much smoke everywhere, I didn't know where to go. I was in the wrong place at the wrong time."

Two other drivers were hospitalized as a result of the accident, but Johnson took the worst of the crash. He sustained a basal skull fracture along with multiple chest and head injuries. At Halifax Medical Center, he was listed as being in extremely critical condition; he was kept alive by a respirator, and he was given medication to help maintain his blood pressure. He was declared brain dead three days later and passed away. The forty-one-year-old Johnson was buried in Florence Memorial Gardens in Florence, South Carolina.

JOE BOOHER

If Joe Booher had been a competitor in team sports, he may have been called a journeyman. Born on February 21, 1941, Booher was a graduate of Purdue University and worked as a farmer and truck driver. Racing was more of a pastime for him, something he enjoyed but did not pursue full time. Throughout his career, he raced in many different series, including ARCA, the Grand National series and the Winston Cup, as it was known at the time. During his Winston Cup career, Joe Booher started twenty-one races and did not qualify for thirteen. For the majority of his races, Booher Farms, his personal business, served as his sponsor. He was no stranger to high-speed tracks, as he qualified at Atlanta, Michigan and the 1980 Daytona 500, where he finished in a respectable seventeenth place, fourteen laps behind the winner, Buddy Baker. Booher scored a career-high finish of eleventh at the 1980 Richmond 400.

Booher arrived in Daytona Beach in 1993 to compete in the Florida 200, a race in the NASCAR Dash Series, a now-defunct series that ran cars that, while they were still fast, were lighter and less powerful than the cars at the top levels of racing. As expected, Booher did not have one of the faster cars on February 12, 1993, and was at the back of the field with several other drivers. Heading into turn one, Booher slid up the track slightly, making contact with the left-front fender of the car driven by Carl Horton. Booher's car then spun into the wall before heading back down the embankment, where it was hit by the oncoming Rodney White.

Driver Ridge Sink had a close-up view of the aftermath: "It happened right in front of me. At first, all I saw was smoke. The smoke kind of cleared, and I saw this mangled racecar. You knew it was bad because his car was really mangled. When I saw them taking him out on the stretcher and I saw the helicopter come down to get him, I said a little prayer." Booher was airlifted to the nearby Halifax Medical Center, where he was pronounced dead from massive internal and head injuries less than forty-five minutes after the start of the race. White was also severely injured but was alert and conscious as he was transported to the hospital via ambulance. He suffered facial cuts and compression fractures to two vertebrae.

The race's winner, Will Hobgood, tried to remain philosophical after the race: "I didn't know what happened; everybody's got in the back of their minds some dangerous things can happen, but when you get in that race car, you've got to put it out of your mind."

NEIL BONNETT AND RODNEY ORR

February 1994 was a month that many in the close-knit world of NASCAR would rather forget. Two drivers, at opposite ends of their careers, both lost their lives in Daytona Beach.

Bonnett was a part of the "Alabama Gang," an informal group that included Bobby, Donnie and Davey Allison, along with driver and crew chief Red Farmer. The men were associated due to their connection to Hueytown, Alabama, a city in north central Alabama that, even today, has only around fifteen thousand residents.

While he was not the flashiest or most successful driver in the series, Neil Bonnett had a career that most drivers would be happy to have. His cup series statistics included 362 starts with 18 wins, 83 top-five finishes and 156 top-ten finishes. He started from the pole twenty times and finished in the top ten in points on three occasions, with a career high of fourth place in 1985. He had a solid career at Daytona International Speedway that included five top-ten finishes in the Daytona 500, three top-ten finishes in the July 400-mile race (including a victory in 1979) and two wins and thirteen top-ten finishes in fifteen starts in the Twin 125-mile qualifying races.

Neil Bonnett was attempting a comeback three years after suffering devastating injuries at the 1990 TransSouth 500 that was held in Darlington. Bonnett was involved in a fourteen-car pileup and ended up slamming into the outside wall with the driver's side of his car. The head injuries he received caused amnesia and a persistent dizziness. He was never able to recall the accident.

Racing was Neil's life, and even though he had a good job working in television as a race analyst after the accident, he still had the urge to drive. In 1992, he began test driving cars for Richard Childress Racing, the car owner for his good friend Dale Earnhardt. In 1993, Childress offered Bonnett the opportunity to return to NASCAR with a seat for the Die Hard 500 to be raced at another extremely fast track, Talladega. About two-thirds of the way through the race, Bonnett was involved in another breath-taking accident. On lap 131, his car spun, became airborne, and eventually made contact with the spectator fence before coming to rest. Miraculously, Bonnett was not severely injured; in fact, he finished the day in the CBS television booth helping call his teammate, Dale Earnhardt's, victory. Bonnett raced one more time in the 1993 season finale in Atlanta, where a blown engine less than ten laps in caused him to finish the race in last place.

The 1994 season started off positively, as Bonnett expected to drive in multiple races. The Country Time Team, which was owned by James Finch and led by crew chief Tony Eury Sr., had high hopes for the season. On the first day of testing, February 11, Bonnett drove the #51 car off pit road. He needed the practice and also needed to shake the car down and see where improvements were needed. A broken shock mount caused him to lose control of his car in turn four. The car headed down to the apron before launching toward the outside retaining wall, hitting it almost directly head on. The forty-seven-year-old Bonnett was killed immediately due to massive head injuries. After a private service, Bonnett was laid to rest at Forest Grove Memorial Gardens in Pleasant Grove, Alabama.

Since his death, Neil Bonnett has received numerous accolades. In 1997, the Alabama Sports Hall of Fame enshrined the racer, as did the National Motorsports Press Association Hall of Fame. Dale Earnhardt dedicated his career-capping 1998 Daytona 500 victory in part to his close friend. In 1998, Bonnett was named one of NASCAR's fifty greatest drivers. In 2001, he was elected to the prestigious Motorsports Hall of Fame. While he has yet to be elected to the NASCAR Hall of Fame, his career statistics show he may very well end up memorialized in Charlotte, North Carolina, in the future.

Only four days after the death of Neil Bonnett, a young racer by the name of Rodney Orr strapped himself into his newly built #37 Ford, sponsored by the Orlando entertainment venue Church Street Station, and he took to the track for a practice run. Rodney Orr was born in Robbinsville, North Carolina, where he began racing on motorcycles. The family then moved to Florida when Rodney's father relocated his construction business there. Orr continued to live in Palm Coast, meaning he had only a short drive south to the speedway. Rodney began racing at local tracks and came up through the Dash Series. As a rookie in 1992, he won "most popular" and "rookie of the year," and in 1993, he won the series title. In his Dash career, he scored two wins, thirteen top-five finishes and twenty-two top-ten finishes in only thirty-five starts. Certainly, this was a strong start to what could be a promising career. He planned to make the jump to what is now the Xfinity Series but, instead, sold his dash car and purchased the pieces he needed to build a cup car. In early practice, the rookie driver exceeded 190 miles per hour at the speedway.

Practice time was essential for a driver like Rodney Orr. He didn't have a lot experience on the big tracks and needed every lap he could get going into qualifying and the Twin 125 qualifying races. As he headed into turn two, Orr lost control of his car, and it spun onto the apron before shooting up to the track. He then flipped upside down before plowing into the outside wall. The rookie driver was pronounced dead on arrival at the Halifax Medical Center. The causes of his death were massive head and upper body injuries. The thirty-one-year-old did not get to try to fulfill his potential. Orr was buried in Lone Oak Cemetery in Graham County, North Carolina.

In an understatement regarding the two closely timed deaths, driver Morgan Shepherd said, "Oh, boy, this is incredible this has happened to us." Car owner Felix Sabates talked of family: "This is a family sport. This young man, we didn't really know who he was, but the fact that he was in the garage running a Winston Cup car, he was part of the family. Our hearts go out to his family." Others, like Kyle Petty, tried to understand the deaths through the danger of the sport, "It's not the first time we've ever come to Daytona and somebody's gotten killed. It's not going to be the last time. It just happens. It's a part of it."

Others were critical of the inexperience of a driver like Rodney Orr. Geoff Bodine voiced an opinion that he and others believed:

> *I think we need to look at the qualifications of drivers, the experience that they have. It should be mandatory that you go so many races on a speedway in a Busch car, and then leave it up to the sanctioning body to say you're ready. No one is doing anything here to see anybody get hurt or killed. We just need to sit down and think about this.*

While Bodine was certainly voicing a valid concern—and one that was no doubt held by many drivers—he was a bit premature when it came to the Rodney Orr accident. While the original cause of the accident was ruled to be Orr's overcorrection after running off the track, experts hired by the *Orlando Sentinel* disagreed. They claimed that a broken shock mount, the same issue that led to the death of Neil Bonnett, caused Orr to lose control of his car. Beacher Orr, Rodney's heartbroken father, expressed relief through his grief. "It wasn't something he did. That's worth a lot. A lot of them thought he was just a rookie who made a rookie mistake."

DALE EARNHARDT SR.

The 2001 death of Dale Earnhardt Sr., probably the most popular NASCAR driver to ever strap on a helmet, is discussed in depth in the chapter "The Best of the Best."

ALAN BURGESS

A racer for many years, Alan Burgess was competing in a Sports Car Club of American (SCCA) event on August 9, 2009, when his GT-2 class Porsche 944 caught fire as it came out of turn four. Burgess coolly navigated his car to pit road, where fire and emergency crews worked to extinguish the flames and pull the driver from the burning car. The fifty-four-year-old Burgess, a facilities director with SYSCO Food Company, suffered severe burns to his hands and face. He was transported to Orlando Regional Hospital that day. While SCCA officials touted the safety features of the cars in their series, including an on-board fire extinguishing system, the burns were more than Burgess could recover from. He passed away on August 28, 2009, as a result of his injuries.

SEE VOLUSIA COUNTY RACING HISTORY FOR YOURSELF

Part of leadership is having the guts to make a decision and then having the guts to stand by it and making it work.
—driver Jeff Burton describing Bill France Jr. and the success of NASCAR

Much of the history of racing in Volusia County can still be seen, with many of the locations being free or of nominal cost to visit. Sure, the beachside has changed dramatically over the years, but you can still walk the track where land speed records were regularly set nearly a century ago. You can walk the route that racers drove before the construction of the Daytona International Speedway. You can tour the speedway that helps create legends, and you can stay at or have drinks at the hotel where NASCAR was born. These and other places can be easily seen today.

BIRTHPLACE OF SPEED PARK AND THE ORMOND GARAGE

The Corner of State Road 40 and A1A
Ormond Beach, Florida

From the very beginning of beach racing it was obvious that the thrill of speed would be a tremendous draw to the Ormond and Daytona Beach area. Fans, both local and from out of town, flocked to the hard-packed sands to watch as man and cars did battle against the clock. It was entrepreneur Henry Flagler who took advantage of this opportunity. Flagler already owned the Florida East Coast Hotel Company, of which the gorgeous Ormond Hotel was a part, along with the Florida East Coast Railway that brought many of the racers and fans to town. Anticipating the continued growth and interest in racing, Flagler built the Ormond Garage in time for the 1904 racing season. Located just east of the Ormond Hotel, the garage served a dual purpose. First, it removed the unsightly image of mechanics working on cars from the hotel grounds. And secondly, Flagler was able to rent out space to racers who enjoyed the convenience of being only blocks away from the beach entry.

The 150-foot-long and 64-foot-wide building had a gabled roof and featured maintenance stalls on both sides with grease pits that had long since been covered. The floor was made of brick, "that [had] borne the tread of the internationally famous in the history of auto racing." In the years after beach racing in the Ormond Beach area ended, the garage was owned by the Oceanside County Club, and it was used as a maintenance and storage facility for the club's electric golf carts. On October 26, 1970, the property was added to the National Register of Historic Places. It was hoped that

Constructed in 1904 by Henry Flagler to accommodate race drivers and their crews who were staying at his Ormond Hotel, the Ormond Garage stood on Granada Avenue until it was gutted by a fire in 1976. *Photograph courtesy of the State Archives of Florida.*

this designation would allow for funding assistance for the upkeep and maintenance of the property.

In the following years, the property's National Register designation deteriorated and at least two attempts were started to purchase and ultimately preserve the structure. A 1970 state proposal estimated the acquisition costs in 1972 to be $50,000, with half of it paid through federal grants and the state covering the other half. The proposal also planned on paying for $10,000 worth of restoration work to be completed in 1973. Those plans never came to life, however.

In 1976, the Ormond Garage caught fire and was burned to the ground. Ormond Garage Company president I.R. Swezey stated, "There's a load of history going up in flames." He was absolutely correct. In addition to the historic structure, four antique cars, an unknown amount of automotive equipment and a tangible link to the early days of automobile racing were lost. All that was left was a state historic marker.

Today, visitors have several sites they can visit along the busy Granada Avenue and A1A route. The state historic marker still stands. It is located in front of the Sun Trust Bank branch located at 113 East Granada Boulevard. The text reads:

> *Built by Flagler East Coast Hotel Company in 1904 for the 1905 races. This landmark in the history of the American automobile industry was the setting for the preparation, testing and servicing of some of the most famous racing cars of the world, which made racing history and records on the nearby beach. It was a proving ground for pioneer automobile manufacturers such as Olds, Winton, Ford and Chevrolet. Some of the famous drivers who made world speed records here were William K. Vanderbilt Jr., Arthur MacDonald, Fred Marriott, Ralph DePalma, Barney Oldfield and Tommy Milton.*

A short walk to the west will bring you to the Ormond Heritage Condominium site. It was here that the Ormond Hotel originally sat. Many of the earliest racecar drivers and crews stayed at the hotel due to its proximity to the beach entrance ramp. Today, the only visible reminder of the Ormond Hotel is the cupola, which can be found in the adjacent Fortunato Park.

Another site associated with the original Ormond Garage is a 1919 structure that served as the engine shop for the original "Birthplace of Speed" Garage. Plans are being made to turn this piece of history into a local craft

This page: The Birthplace of Speed Park, located at the corner of Granada Boulevard and A1A, serves as a reminder of the early days of beach racing and its importance in local history. *Author's collection.*

brewery and restaurant. The owners and managers of other successful local eateries are behind the plans. They plan to keep as much of the original detailing of the building as possible while offering a modern menu and a potential for live music. Discussions have also taken place to include a replica of the 1906 Stanley Steamer Rocket in the brewery.

A final destination for those who want to have a feel of the early racing in Ormond Beach is the Ormond Garage replica, which is housed in the Birthplace of Speed Park. Located at the eastern terminus of SR 40, the small park includes a downsized version of the original Ormond Garage. The garage was funded by the Motor Racing Heritage Network, and the park was dedicated on March 28, 2013. In addition to the garage replica, there are several monuments commemorating various aspects of beach racing.

DAYTONA INTERNATIONAL SPEEDWAY

1801 West International Speedway
Daytona Beach, Florida 32114

Often called the "World Center of Racing," Daytona International Speedway is a must-visit for any fan of auto racing. Whether the vehicles were open-wheel, closed-wheel, prototypes or carts, they had a history here at the massive track. The best way to take it all in is to take one of the tours that are offered. There are several different tours of varying lengths, depths and prices. No matter your interest level, a tour will give you the opportunity to see the track up close and personal as you travel on the high banks, visit Victory Lane, see the actual car that won the most recent Daytona 500 and end with a tour of the Motorsports Hall of Fame of America, which features displays of memorabilia of all types from racing.

"Big Bill" France began making plans for the speedway in the years after the formation of NASCAR. Construction began on the track in 1957, with a groundbreaking taking place in November. Construction costs were high, and France had to come up with funding. He borrowed more than $600,000, secured sponsorships and also sold three hundred thousand shares of stock to provide the capital needed. France wanted to have high banking on the track. This would not only afford spectators better views but would also allow

Daytona International Speedway is host to numerous events throughout the year, including NASCAR races, motorcycle races, endurance races, concerts, car shows and more. *Author's collection.*

drivers to increase their speeds. In order to build the banking, ground was dug from the infield to help build up the corners. This digging eventually helped create the picturesque Lake Lloyd that now graces the infield.

By February 1959, the track was ready for testing. The first official race held at the speedway was the Daytona 500 on February 22, 1959. Racing was moved from the sand-and-road course to the new high-banked track that afforded drivers a new challenge and higher speeds. Attendance for the first Daytona 500 was 41,921.

The first Daytona 500 was everything France could have asked for. Pole-sitter Bob Welborn led fifty-nine cars to the green flag for the start of the race. Welborn's day ended after only seventy-five laps with a blown engine; he finished in forty-first place. As the race laps wore down, there were two drivers on the lead lap: Johnny Beauchamp and Lee Petty. Beauchamp had not won in the series and was only starting his seventh race. Petty had won nearly forty races. The ending was a photo finish. Lee Petty claimed, "I had Beauchamp by a good two feet. In my own mind, I know I won." Beauchamp believed he took the checkered flag. "I had him by two feet. I glanced over to Lee Petty's car as I crossed the finish line, and I could see his headlight slightly back of my car." Legendary racer Fireball Roberts, who exited the

Here, we see Ms. Daytona 1959 waving to fans before the start of the inaugural Daytona 500. *Photograph courtesy of the State Archives of Florida, photographer Francis P. Johnson.*

An aerial view of Daytona International Speedway shows just how large the complex is. The large body of water is Lake Lloyd. It came into existence because of the massive amounts of earth that were removed to create the high banks in the turns. *Photograph courtesy of the State Archives of Florida.*

race with a faulty fuel pump, called the race for Petty. On Monday, the newspaper headlines read, "Beauchamp Wins—Unofficially." Bill France and NASCAR officials huddled for three days, reviewing photographs and newsreel footage, before declaring Lee Petty the official winner—three days of incredible publicity for the track and the series.

As is expected for any entertainment facility, changes and upgrades have been made throughout the years. In 1998, lights were installed, and now, each year, the second Daytona Cup race of the season is held under the lights. In July 2013, the Daytona Rising Project was started. This three-year project removed the track's backstretch seating and renovated the seating along the front stretch. The project cost around $400 million and improved not just seating but included more entrances that were easier to access for fans, better concession areas and improved restroom facilities. Currently, there is seating for 101,500 spectators.

This page: Situated outside Daytona International Speedway are these large sculptures of the two men who have had the most influence on NASCAR: Bill France Sr. (with his wife, Anne) and Bill France Jr. *Both photographs are courtesy of the author.*

Outside the speedway, there are several areas that are worth noting. There are sculptures of Bill France Sr., Annie B. France, Bill France Jr. and Dale Earnhardt Sr. All of them were crafted by artist John Lajba, a sculptor based in Omaha, Nebraska, who has almost legendary status in Daytona Beach. In addition to his work for the speedway, he has also sculpted the likeness of Mary McLeod Bethune; that sculpture proudly sits on the campus of Bethune-Cookman University. Each year, Lajba casts the miniature version of the Harley J. Earl Trophy that is awarded to the winner of the Daytona 500.

While admiring the sculptures, you can also walk through the Daytona 500 Champions' Walk of Fame. This is Daytona's version of the Hollywood Walk of Fame, only here, you have to have won the biggest NASCAR race of all to be included. Winners of the Daytona 500, starting with Dale Jarrett in 1996, have been immortalized with hand- and footprints set in concrete for visitors to measure up against.

STREAMLINE HOTEL

140 South Atlantic Avenue
Daytona Beach, Florida 32118

Located along Atlantic Avenue, the beautiful Streamline Hotel has been brought to a level of opulence that only a few short years ago would have been completely unimaginable. The current principal owner of the Streamline is Eddie Hennesey, the son of Phillippe and Sylvie Hennesey, the founders of the cosmetic company Pevonia International. He purchased the hotel in 2014 for $950,000. In the ensuing years, he has put a considerable amount of blood, sweat, tears and cash—approximately $6 million—into the historic structure, which now provides visitors with the unique opportunity to stay in the building where NASCAR came to life. You may also want a bite to eat or a drink; if so, you should visit the rooftop bar or stop at Olivier's Hideaway.

Built around 1940, the Streamline was designed by Alan MacDonough, a prominent Florida architect, and was constructed in what is called the Streamline Moderne style of architecture. This style features flowing curves, flat roofs and long horizontal lines, and it often used nautical elements. The style was also used in household appliances, such as toasters and telephones, along with larger transportation related items, like buses and railroad locomotives.

Opening just before World War II, the hotel offered accommodations for members of the Women's Auxiliary Army Corp (WAACs). With the hotel being considered fireproof and strong enough to be used as a bomb shelter, it made a perfect home for these ladies. Legend says that a criminal element was operating out of the hotel in the early days. Stories are told that gangsters used the hotel safe to hide cash, and it is said that a hidden tunnel offered an escape route to the beach. During the extensive renovations, Masonic symbols were found around the building.

It was in the hotel's Ebony Room Rooftop Bar that Bill France Sr. began meeting with drivers, car owners and other connected officials to discuss the issues related to racing in December 1947. A local journalist called it "racing's equivalent of our nation's Constitutional Convention." Bill France Sr. kicked off the meeting by saying, "Right here, within our group, rests the outcome of stock car racing in the country today. We have the opportunity to set it up on a big scale." France and the others settled on a consistent set of rules, along with national standings, setting the standard for NASCAR racing as it is known today. By February 21, 1948, they had

This page: The Streamline Hotel, located on A1A in Daytona Beach, is where Bill France Sr. and others put together the framework of what is now NASCAR. *Both photographs courtesy of the author.*

hammered out an agreement, creating the National Stock Car Racing Association, later to be named NASCAR.

In the years afterward, the Streamline went through several reincarnations. It has served as a hotel, youth hostel, a religious retirement home and a gay-friendly hotel and bar that regularly featured weekend drag shows. As so often happens with properties such as this one, particularly when they are in an economically depressed location, the hotel declined significantly. The property was in poor condition, and the police were regularly on site, dealing with various illegal activities. In 2014, a new owner, Eddie Hennessy, stepped in with plans to bring the property back to life as a boutique hotel. Having paid just under $1 million dollars for the property, Hennessy and his partners invested approximately $6 million into bringing the property up to the high standards it has today. Visitors may now book a room, have dinner at Olivier's Hideaway restaurant and head up to the rooftop bar for an evening party with incredible sunset views.

RACING'S NORTH TURN

4511 South Atlantic Avenue
Ponce Inlet, Florida 32127

In addition to providing good meals, drinks and a relaxing environment with a beach view, Racing's North Turn sits at a historical location. It was here that race fans of the 1930s through the late 1950s could see cars leave the sands of the beach, only to speed down the pavement of Atlantic Avenue on what was to become a track that was just over four miles in length.

Visitors to the restaurant are treated to a collection of racing memorabilia, and the restaurant has something for everybody. From paper items to trophies, steering wheels, race helmets and a car that greets you at the front door, owners Rhonda and Walter Glasnak have it all displayed. Rhonda Glasnak stated this in an interview with Daytona International Speedway: "It's really important to me to make sure that we tell a story. We've worked really hard to do so, and I think we've been successful. On any day that we're open, you'll find people in here just walking around. Some people don't even eat."

While patrons today would never realize it, the landmark was almost lost to a fire in 2014. An overnight kitchen fire caused terrible damage, including

This page: Racing's North Turn Restaurant is located where racers in the Daytona Beach and Road Course event would exit the beach and speed south before turning onto the sands again. *Author's collection.*

the loss of the incredible artifact collection. After more than six weeks of work, the restaurant was able to open on a limited basis, working out of a food truck. Thanks to the owners' continued hard work, the support of the Town of Ponce Inlet and the generosity of locals who helped replenish the lost collection, Racing's North Turn remains a vibrant part of the community today.

During race weeks, it is common to see many veterans of racing participate in the annual North Turn Legends Beach Parade. This celebration brings out the best in the community, as attendees watch cars and drivers of yesterday drive the old beach circuit. The event is held every February.

DAYTONA MEMORIAL PARK CEMETERY

1425 Bellevue Road
Daytona Beach, Florida 32114

Near the roar of the speedway and on the flight path for planes both large and small is Daytona Memorial Park Cemetery. This fairly large cemetery, which is home to more than twenty-five thousand plots, features the grave sites of several famous individuals, including baseball players Fred Merkle and Napolean Lajoie and Florida governor David Sholtz. The cemetery's connection to NASCAR includes the grave sites of Fireball Roberts and Bill France Jr. and his wife, Betty, which are easy to find.

It is important to note that Daytona Memorial is located on both the north and south sides of Bellevue Road. You will need to enter on the south side of Bellevue, the side with the main offices. On entry, you should take the left fork. While traveling through the cemetery, be on the lookout for a large, above-ground multiburial vault on your left-hand side (or the east side of the cemetery). On the top of this vault, you will notice a large open Bible. There, you will find the burial location of Edward Glenn "Fireball" Roberts.

Roberts was born in nearby Tavares, Florida, and early on, he took an interest in both auto racing and baseball. It was through his pitching that he earned the nickname "Fireball." In 1950, at the age of only twenty-one, he raced in the Grand National beach-and-road race in Daytona. He completed only eight laps and finished in a distant thirty-third place.

This page: "Fireball" Roberts earned his nickname for his baseball abilities and not his racing. Roberts is interred in Daytona Memorial Park in this easy-to-find above-ground vault. *Both photographs are courtesy of the author.*

Seated in this his #22 racecar is Glenn "Fireball" Roberts. In 206 NASCAR cup-level starts, Roberts won an amazing thirty-three races, including the 1963 Daytona 500. *Photograph courtesy of the State Archives of Florida.*

With the opening of the new Daytona International Speedway in 1959, Roberts took his skills to the new high-banked track. The first Daytona 500 was not a positive one for Roberts, as he started in the forty-sixth position and finished in forty-fifth after a fuel pump issue put him behind the wall after only fifty-six laps. However, better years were to come for Roberts. Driving a car built by legendary mechanic Smokey Yunick, Roberts started from the pole in the Daytona 500 three times, from 1961 to 1963. He won the race in 1962. He came back to Daytona in July 1962 and won the Firecracker race as well. He won the Firecracker again in 1963. In his career, he won 33 races in 206 starts. He finished in the top ten an incredible 122 times.

Unfortunately, his career was cut short. On May 24, 1964, at the World 600, Roberts crashed while trying to avoid an accident that involved Ned Jarrett and Junior Johnson. His Ford hit the inside retaining wall, flipped and caught on fire. Jarrett ran to his aid and pulled him from the burning wreckage. Roberts suffered second- and third-degree burns over 80 percent of his body. Roberts clung to life, and it was thought he might be able to pull through. However, two weeks after the crash, he contracted pneumonia and sepsis. He slipped into a coma and passed away on July 2, 1964.

Fireball Roberts received many accolades after his untimely passing. He was named one of NASCAR's Fifty Greatest Drivers, and he was elected to the International Motorsports Hall of Fame, the Motorsports Hall of Fame of America, the Florida Sports Hall of Fame and, perhaps most impressively, the NASCAR Hall of Fame in 2014.

Also, following the left-entrance fork, continue to drive; then, you will see a man-made lake with several above-ground mausoleums. There, you will find the France Mausoleum. Bill France Jr. started his career in the racing industry doing whatever was needed. His obituary stated that, in addition to working crowd control at beach races, "he also was a flagman, sold concessions, parked cars, scored races, promoted events, and even helped in the construction of Daytona International Speedway." In 1972, when he took over as chairman of NASCAR from his father, he knew the workings of the sport. He understood his audience and also knew that the sport needed to expand to reach its full potential.

Bill France Jr. is most often credited with taking the regional sport and bringing it to the wider attention of America. Richard Petty summed this up well:

> *His dad started it, got it up and running, and Junior took it and put the people together to take it from a southern sport to a national sport. He was there when it was developed with the TV, when it was developed with the new cars, when it was developed from half-mile dirt tracks to superspeedways. You just look at the popularity and look at the people and look at the money involved—he must have done a heck of a job at it.*

France Jr. understood the financial potential of NASCAR and worked to exploit it for the benefit of all involved. When he took over, NASCAR races were only shown in pieces on tape delay. In 1979, he reached a deal with CBS Sports to televise the Daytona 500 live. The race was a huge success for both NASCAR and CBS. A snowstorm in the northeast kept people cooped up in their houses with little to entertain them in the pre-internet and limited-television-channel days. Also, the race was exciting, and the postrace fight between Cale Yarborough and the Allison brothers brought a new wave of fans to the sport. By 1999, France and NASCAR

Bill France Jr. is credited with taking NASCAR from being a sport with regional interest to one of national and worldwide importance. France passed away in 2007 and was laid to rest in this mausoleum in Daytona Memorial Park. *Author's collection.*

had signed a $2.4 billion television deal, with races being shown on multiple networks beginning in 2001. NASCAR currently has television deals valued at more than $8 billion that will take them to the year 2024. In summarizing France's business acumen, driver Jeff Burton said, "His role in the impact of the sport has been huge. His personality came at a time when it was what our sport needed."

France, who had suffered with multiple health issues in his later years, passed the racing torches to son Brian and daughter Lesa. France passed away June 4, 2007, at the age of seventy-four. His wife, Betty Jane, who helped found the NASCAR Foundation, an organization dedicated to children's healthcare, and who served as the executive vice president of NASCAR, passed away in 2016.

Also interred at Daytona Memorial Park are legendary engine builder and car owner Raymond Fox and Marshall Teague, the driver who passed away as the result of a testing accident at Daytona International Speedway.

HILLSIDE CEMETERY

143 Seton Trail
Ormond Beach, Florida 32176

Situated in a quiet residential neighborhood is Hillside Cemetery. Serving as the final resting spot for more than three thousand people, Hillside is a quiet, well-taken-care-of cemetery. Its grave sites include those of local settlers, veterans of multiple wars and prominent families. Among the prominent people buried here are Bill and Annie France. The France's are buried under a marker that gives no indication to Bill's association to racing. If you didn't know who he was, you probably would not give the marker a second look.

Bill France Sr., along with fellow drivers, car owners and others in the sport met in 1947 at the Streamline Hotel, ultimately founding NASCAR. In 1953, he proposed building a speedway, and in 1956, ground broke on Daytona International Speedway. The track opened in 1959. France and his son Bill Jr. were both inducted to the NASCAR Hall of Fame as part of the inaugural group in 2010.

The France family marker can easily be found. On entering the cemetery, you will note that there is a black metal fence. There, park your car. When facing the entrance and the fencing, walk to your right. To the right of the right-hand entrance road, you will find the France marker in the row nearest the fence.

Giving no indication to his fame or place in history, Bill France Sr. and his wife, Anne, are buried in Hillside Cemetery, which is located beachside in Ormond Beach. The marker is located near the north entrance of the cemetery along the first row of headstones. *Author's collection.*

LIVING LEGENDS OF AUTO RACING MUSEUM

2400 South Ridgewood Avenue (Located in the Sunshine Mall)
South Daytona, Florida 32119

Located in the Sunshine Mall, the Living Legends of Auto Racing Museum is a must-visit for any fan of racing. The museum features a rotating collection of cars, with some being on display in the mall itself during race weeks. Also on display are hundreds of archival photographs along with memorabilia, such as helmets, trophies and articles of clothing from racers whose names you will easily recognize and those who perhaps only diehard fans will remember.

Operated by the Living Legends of Auto Racing Inc., a 501(c)(3) organization, the museum hosts and participates in many events throughout the year. During Speedweeks, it hosts talks and autograph sessions with drivers from all forms of racing, it offers presentations to groups and organizations in the area and it holds regular car shows. The group is also behind the Living Legends of Auto Racing Memorial Brick Walk of Fame that is located at 3050 South Atlantic Avenue in Daytona Beach Shores.

The museum is free and open to the public. Donations are, of course, welcomed to help cover operating expenses. You can also join LLAR for a nominal annual fee. For those interested in the history of auto racing, this is a group you should consider joining.

NEW SMYRNA SPEEDWAY

3939 State Road 44
New Smyrna Beach, Florida 32168

For those wanting to see local short-track action, you can't miss out on the New Smyrna Speedway. This track is a high-banked, half-mile paved oval that challenges drivers of all skill levels in all categories of racing. The track originally opened as a dirt track in 1967 but was soon paved in order to hold the World Series of Stock Car Races, which is held during the annual February Speedweeks. The grandstand's seating capacity is eight thousand.

The track is considered to be quite a challenge, and big-name drivers, like Kyle Busch, Ryan Newman, Tony Stewart and others, have competed there.

As nine-time NASCAR National Modified Champion and 2011 NASCAR Hall of Fame inductee Richie Evans said, "If you can win at New Smyrna Speedway, you can win anywhere in the United States."

Today, the track regularly hosts the Late-Model, Bombers, Trucks and Sportsmen Series races. Special event races are held throughout the year, and the track serves as the season kick-off point for the NASCAR K&N Pro Series's East Series. Tickets are generally under twenty dollars per person, and the speedway strives to make this a fun venue for the entire family.

DAYTONA 500 WINNERS

1959	February 22	Lee Petty
1960	February 24	Junior Johnson
1961	February 26	Marvin Panch
1962	February 18	Fireball Roberts
1963	February 24	Tiny Lund
1964	February 23	Richard Petty
1965	February 14	Fred Lorenzen[*]
1966	February 27	Richard Petty[*]
1967	February 26	Mario Andretti[†]
1968	February 25	Cale Yarborough
1969	February 23	LeeRoy Yarbrough
1970	February 22	Pete Hamilton
1971	February 14	Richard Petty
1972	February 20	A.J. Foyt
1973	February 18	Richard Petty
1974	February 17	Richard Petty
1975	February 16	Benny Parsons
1976	February 15	David Pearson
1977	February 20	Cale Yarborough
1978	February 19	Bobby Allison
1979	February 18	Richard Petty

1980	February 17	Buddy Baker
1981	February 15	Richard Petty
1982	February 14	Bobby Allison
1983	February 20	Cale Yarborough
1984	Febraury 19	Cale Yarborough
1985	February 17	Bill Elliott
1986	February 16	Geoffrey Bodine
1987	February 15	Bill Elliott
1988	February 14	Bobby Allison
1989	February 19	Darrell Waltrip
1990	February 18	Derrike Cope
1991	February 17	Ernie Irvan
1992	February 16	Davey Allison
1993	February 14	Dale Jarrett
1994	February 20	Sterling Marlin
1995	February 19	Sterling Marlin
1996	February 18	Dale Jarrett
1997	February 16	Jeff Gordon
1998	February 15	Dale Earnhardt
1999	February 14	Jeff Gordon
2000	February 20	Dale Jarrett
2001	February 18	Michael Waltrip
2002	February 17	Ward Burton
2003	February 16	Michael Waltrip*
2004	February 15	Dale Earnhardt Jr.
2005	February 20	Jeff Gordon
2006	February 19	Jimmie Johnson
2007	February 18	Kevin Harvick
2008	February 17	Ryan Newman
2009	February 15	Matt Kenseth*
2010	February 14	Jamie McMurray
2011	February 20	Trevor Bayne‡
2012	February 28	Matt Kenseth
2013	February 24	Jimmie Johnson
2014	February 23	Dale Earnhardt Jr.
2015	February 22	Joey Logano
2016	February 21	Denny Hamlin
2017	February 26	Kurt Busch

2018	February 18	Austin Dillon
2019	February 17	Denny Hamlin
2020	February 16	Denny Hamlin

* Race shortened due to rain.

† Mario Andretti is the only foreign-born driver to have won the Daytona 500.

‡ Trevor Bayne is the youngest winner of the Daytona 500, as he won the race at only twenty years and one day old.

DAYTONA 500 MULTITIME WINNERS

Allison, Bobby	1978, 1982, 1988
Earnhardt, Dale, Jr.	2004, 2014
Elliott, Bill	1985, 1987
Gordon, Jeff	1997, 1999, 2005
Hamlin, Denny	2016, 2019, 2020
Jarrett, Dale	1993, 1996, 2000
Johnson, Jimmie	2006, 2013
Kenseth, Matt	2009, 2012
Marlin, Sterling	1994, 1995
Petty, Richard	1964, 1966, 1971, 1973, 1974, 1979, 1981
Waltrip, Michael	2001, 2003
Yarborough, Cale	1968, 1977, 1983, 1984

FIRECRACKER AND COKE ZERO 400 WINNERS

1959*	July 4	Fireball Roberts
1960	July 4	Jack Smith
1961	July 4	David Pearson
1962	July 4	Fireball Roberts
1963	July 4	Fireball Roberts
1964	July 4	A.J. Foyt
1965	July 4	A.J. Foyt
1966	July 4	Sam McQuagg
1967	July 4	Cale Yarborough
1968	July 4	Cale Yarborough
1969	July 4	LeeRoy Yarbrough
1970	July 4	Donnie Allison
1971	July 4	Bobby Isaac
1972	July 4	David Pearson
1973	July 4	David Pearson
1974	July 4	David Pearson
1975	July 4	Richard Petty
1976	July 4	Cale Yarborough
1977*	July 4	Richard Petty
1978	July 4	David Pearson
1979	July 4	Neil Bonnett

1980	July 4	Bobby Allison
1981	July 4	Cale Yarborough
1982	July 4	Bobby Allison
1983	July 4	Buddy Baker
1984	July 4	Richard Petty
1985	July 4	Greg Sacks
1986	July 4	Tim Richmond
1987	July 4	Bobby Allison
1988[†]	July 2	Bill Elliott
1989	July 1	Davey Allison
1990	July 7	Dale Earnhardt
1991	July 6	Bill Elliott
1992	July 4	Ernie Irvan
1993	July 3	Dale Earnhardt
1994	July 2	Jimmy Spencer
1995	July 1	Jeff Gordon
1996	July 6	Sterling Marlin
1997	July 5	John Andretti
1998[‡]	October 17	Jeff Gordon
1999	July 3	Dale Jarrett
2000	July 1	Jeff Burton
2001	July 7	Dale Earnhardt Jr.
2002	July 6	Michael Waltrip
2003	July 5	Greg Biffle
2004	July 3–4[§]	Jeff Gordon
2005	July 2–3[§]	Tony Stewart
2006	July 1	Tony Stewart
2007	July 7	Jamie McMurray
2008	July 5	Kyle Busch
2009	July 4	Tony Stewart
2010	July 3–4[§]	Kevin Harvick
2011	July 2	David Ragan
2012	July 7	Tony Stewart
2013	July 6	Jimmie Johnson
2014	July 6	Aric Almirola
2015	July 5–6[§]	Dale Earnhardt Jr.
2016	July 2	Brad Keselowski
2017	July 1	Ricky Stenhouse Jr.

2018	July 7	Erik Jones
2019‖	July 6–7§	Justin Haley
2020	August 29	William Byron

* From 1959 to 1962, the race was only 250 miles long. It was extended by 150 miles in 1963.

† Prior to 1988, the race had been run on July 4. Beginning in 1988, the race was scheduled for the first Saturday in July. The year 1988 also marked the last year that the race was called the Firecracker 400.

‡ During July 1998, the state of Florida was hit by disastrous wildfires, and the track was used as a staging area for firefighters. The race was rescheduled for October and became the first NASCAR race in Daytona Beach to be run under lights. The race is now scheduled during the evening in order to avoid the summer heat and afternoon rainstorms.

§ These races were run over two days due to weather issues.

‖ The year 2019 was the final year the Daytona 400 was run in July. NASCAR made the decision to move the race to late August, when it will become the final race in "regular season" before the beginning of the ten-race playoff for the championship. Daytona International Speedway now kicks off and holds the final race of the regular season.

FIRECRACKER AND COKE ZERO 400 MULTITIME WINNERS

Allison, Bobby	1980, 1982, 1987
Earnhardt, Dale, Sr.	1990, 1993
Earnhardt, Dale, Jr.	2001, 2015
Elliott, Bill	1988, 1991
Foyt, A.J.	1964, 1965
Gordon, Jeff	1995, 1998, 2004
Pearson, David	1961, 1972, 1973, 1974, 1978
Petty, Richard	1975, 1977, 1984
Roberts, Fireball	1959, 1962, 1963
Stewart, Tony	2005, 2006, 2009, 2012
Yarborough, Cale	1967, 1968, 1976, 1981

DAYTONA 300 WINNERS

The Daytona 300 is the first race in the NASCAR Infinity Series. This race traces its origins to when NASCAR ran on the hard-packed sands of Daytona Beach (1948–58). It was a part of the Modified Series and later the Modified and Sportsman Series. The race has traditionally been run the day before the Grand National Series, now known as the Monster Energy NASCAR Cup Series. This race has been run under multiple sponsor names and, as such, the generic Daytona 300 name is used here.

1948	February 15	Red Byron
	August 8	Fonty Flock
1949	January 16	Marshall Teague
1950	February 4	Gober Sosebee
1951	February 10	Gober Sosebee
1952	February 9	Tim Flock
1953	February 14	Cotton Owens
1954	February 20	Cotton Owens
1955	February 26	Banjo Matthews
1956	February 24	Tim Flock
1957	February 15	Speedy Thompson
1958	February 21	Banjo Matthews
1959	February 21	Banjo Matthews
1960	February 13	Bubba Farr

1961	February 25	Jimmy Thompson
1962	February 17	Lee Roy Yarbrough
1963	February 23	Lee Roy Yarbrough
1964	February 22	Tiny Lund
1965	February 13	Marvin Panch
1966	February 27	Curtis Turner
1967	February 25	Jim Paschal
1968	February 24	Bunkie Blackburn
1969*	February 22	Lee Roy Yarbrough
1970	February 21	Tiny Lund
1971	February 13	Red Farmer
1972	February 19	Bill Dennis
1973	February 17	Bill Dennis
1974	February 16	Bill Dennis
1975	February 15	Jack Ingram
1976	February 14	Joe Millikan
1977	February 19	Donnie Allison
1978	February 18	Darrell Waltrip
1979	February 17	Darrell Waltrip
1980	February 16	Jack Ingram
1981	February 14/16*	David Pearson
1982	February 13	Dale Earnhardt
1983	February 19	Darrell Waltrip
1984	February 18	Darrell Waltrip
1985	February 16	Geoffrey Bodine
1986	February 15	Dale Earnhardt
1987	February 14	Geoffrey Bodine
1988	February 13	Bobby Allison
1989	February 18	Darrell Waltrip
1990	February 17	Dale Earnhardt
1991	February 16	Dale Earnhardt
1992	February 15	Dale Earnhardt
1993	February 13	Dale Earnhardt
1994	February 19	Dale Earnhardt
1995	February 18	Chad Little
1996	February 17	Steve Grissom
1997	February 15	Randy LaJoie
1998	February 14	Joe Nemechek
1999	February 13	Randy LaJoie

2000	February 19	Matt Kenseth
2001	February 17	Randy LaJoie
2002	February 16	Dale Earnhardt Jr.
2003	February 15	Dale Earnhardt Jr.
2004	February 14/16*	Dale Earnhardt Jr.
2005	February 19	Tony Stewart
2006	February 18	Tony Stewart
2007	February 17	Kevin Harvick
2008	February 16	Tony Stewart
2009	February 14	Tony Stewart
2010	February 13	Tony Stewart
2011	February 19	Tony Stewart
2012	February 25	James Buescher
2013	February 23	Tony Stewart
2014	February 22	Regan Smith
2015	February 21	Ryan Reed
2016	February 20	Chase Elliott
2017	February 25	Ryan Reed
2018	February 17	Tyler Reddick†
2019	February 16	Michael Annett
2020	February 15	Noah Gragson

* The 1981 and 2004 races were started on Saturday and finished on Monday due to rain.

† Tyler Reddick defeated Elliot Sadler at the start and finish line by only .00004 seconds, or less than three inches—the closest finish in NASCAR history.

DAYTONA 300 MULTITIME WINNERS

Bodine, Geoffrey	1985, 1987
Dennis, Bill	1972, 1973, 1974
Earnhardt, Dale, Sr.	1982, 1986, 1990, 1991, 1992, 1993, 1994
Earnhardt, Dale, Jr.	2002, 2003, 2004
Flock, Tim	1952, 1956
Ingram, Jack	1975, 1980
LaJoie, Randy	1997, 1999, 2001
Lund, Tiny	1964, 1970
Matthews, Banjo	1955, 1958, 1959
Owens, Cotton	1953, 1954
Reed, Ryan	2015, 2017
Sosebee, Gober	1950, 1951
Stewart, Tony	2005, 2006, 2008, 2009, 2010, 2011, 2013
Waltrip, Darrell	1978, 1979, 1983, 1984, 1989
Yarbrough, LeeRoy	1962, 1963, 1969

NEXTERA ENERGY RESOURCES 250 WINNERS (TRUCKS)

This race is the first of the NASCAR Camping World Truck Series each season and is traditionally held on Friday evening, with the first night race having been held in 2004.

2000	February 18	Mike Wallace
2001	February 16*	Joe Ruttman
2002	February 15	Robert Pressley
2003	February 14*	Rick Crawford
2004	February 13	Carl Edwards
2005	February 18	Bobby Hamilton
2006	February 17*	Mark Martin
2007	February 16	Jack Sprague
2008	February 15	Todd Bodine
2009	February 13	Todd Bodine
2010	February 13†	Timothy Peters
2011	February 18*	Michael Waltrip
2012	February 24*	John King
2013	February 22	Johnny Sauter
2014	February 21	Kyle Busch
2015	February 20	Tyler Reddick
2016	February 19	Johnny Sauter
2017	February 24	Kaz Grala
2018	February 16	Johnny Sauter

2019	February 15*	Austin Hill
2020	February 14	Grant Enfinger

* Race extended due to NASCAR overtime rules.

† Postponed from February 12.

AUTO RACING–RELATED DEATHS IN DAYTONA BEACH

BEACH RACING

Frank Croker, January 21, 1905
    Timed trial run
Frank Lockhart, April 25, 1928
    Land speed record attempt
Lee Bible, March 13, 1929
    Land speed record attempt

RACING DEATHS AT DAYTONA INTERNATIONAL SPEEDWAY

Marshall Teague, February 11, 1959
    Closed course speed record attempt
George Amick, April 4, 1959
    Daytona 100 United States Auto Club (USAC) race
Habe Haberling, February 21, 1961
    250-mile race practice
Don MacTavash, February 22, 1969
    Permatex 300

Tab Prince, February 1970
  125-mile qualifier race
David Pearl, July 31, 1971
  Sports Car Club of America (SCCA) Paul Whiteman Trophy race
Friday Hassler, February 17, 1972
  125-mile qualifier race
Ricky Knotts, February 14, 1980
  125-mile qualifier race
Francis Affleck, February 7, 1985
  Automobile Racing Club of America (ARCA) Daytona ARCA 200
Bruce Jacobi, injured February 17, 1983, died February 4, 1987
  125-mile qualifier race
Joe Young, February 13, 1987
  Komfort Koach 200 NASCAR Dash Series
Don Williams, injured February 17, 1979, died May 21, 1989
  Sportsman 300
Julius "Slick" Johnson, February 11, 1990
  Automobile Racing Club of America (ARCA) Daytona ARCA 200
Joe Booher, February 12, 1993
  Florida 200 race NASCAR Dash Series
Neil Bonnett, February 11, 1994
  Daytona 500 practice
Rodney Orr, February 14, 1994
  Daytona 500 practice
Dale Earnhardt Sr., February 18, 2001
  Daytona 500 race
Alan Burgess, August 9, 2009
  Sports Car Club of America (SCCA) Daytona Double SARRC

BIBLIOGRAPHY

Books and Articles

Cardwell, Harold, Sr. *Daytona Beach: 100 Years of Racing (Images of America)*. Charleston, SC: Arcadia Publishing, 2002.

———. "Racing on the Sand at Daytona Beach." *Halifax Herald* 12, no. 1 (June 1996): 15–17.

Guthrie, Janet. *A Life at Full Throttle*. Toronto: Sport Media Publishing, 2005.

Hebel, Ianthe Bond, ed. *Centennial History of Volusia County, Florida 1854–1954*. Daytona Beach, FL: College Publishing Company, 1955.

Houston, Rick. *Dale vs. Daytona: The Intimidator's Quest to Win the Great American Race*. Forest Lake, MN: CarTech Inc., 2017.

Lynn, Thomas. "The Ormond Garage: America's First Gasoline Alley." *Halifax Herald*, 31, no. 1 (Winter 2013): 8–12.

Merrick, H. James. *Bravo, Stanley! The Racing History of Stanley and the 1906 Stanley Land Speed Record*. Kingfield, ME: Stanley Museum Inc., 2006.

Punnett, Dick. *Beach Racing: Daytona Before Nascar*. Gainesville: University Press of Florida, 2008.

———. *Racing on the Rim: A History of the Annual Automobile Racing Tournaments Held on the Sands of the Ormond-Daytona Beach, Florida; 1903–1910*. Ormond Beach, FL: Tomoka Press, 1997.

Schene, Michael G. *Hopes, Dreams, and Promises: A History of Volusia County, Florida*. Daytona Beach, FL: News-Journal Corporation, 1976.

Strickland, Alice. "Florida's Golden Age of Racing." *Florida Historical Quarterly*, 45, no. 3 (January 1967): 253–69.

Taylor, Virgil. "Knight of Speed: Sir Henry Seagrave and the 1929 Land Speed Record Trials." *Halifax Herald*, 36, no. 1 (Spring 2018).

———. "The 25th Anniversary World Speed Record Trials and 'Wonder Boy' Frank Lockhart." *Halifax Herald*, 34, no. 1 (Summer 2016).

Tuthill, William R. *Speed on Sand: The Story of Motor Racing and Record Breaking at the Birthplace of Speed; 1903–1959 Revised Edition.* Ormond Beach, FL: Ormond Beach Historical Trust Inc., 2002.

Waltrip, Michael. *In the Blink of an Eye: Dale, Daytona, and the Day That Changed Everything.* New York: Hyperion, 2011.

Websites

Al Blixt Racing History

BBC News

California Digital Newspaper Collection

Encyclopedia of Alabama

ESPN

Florida Master Site File Index

Florida Memory Project

Fox Sports

Georgia Racing Hall of Fame

Janet Guthrie

Jennifer Jo Cobb

JR Motorsports

Laurens County Sports History

Legacy

Living Legends of Auto Racing

Marshal Teague

NBC Sports

New Smyrna Speedway

Newseum

Racing-Reference

SpeedSport

Journals, Magazines and Newspapers

Daytona Beach News Journal
Grand National Scene
Halifax Herald
Indianapolis Star
Orlando Sentinel
Sacramento Union
Spartanburg Herald-Journal
USA Today

Miscellaneous

Certificate of Appropriateness Application DEV2014-119 Streamline Hotel Restoration. Application dated October 13, 2014, and provided to Daytona Beach Historic Preservation board members from Reed Berger, redevelopment director.

Elliott, Jeremy. Bruce Jacobi (1935–1987) manuscript typescript provided to author.

Official Accident Report, No. 3 Car, August 21, 2001. This is the official NASCAR report with findings from NASCAR, Biodynamic Research Corporation and the University of Nebraska.

Official Program Ormond-Daytona Beach Races, January 25 to February 6, 1904. State Library of Florida: Florida Collection, 796.72-F636 01. www.floridamemory.com.

Ormond Garage. Florida Master Site File, file #VO211. Florida Division of Historical Resources.

Stanley Land Speed Record Centennial 1906–2006 Press Kit. www.ormondbeach.org.

Streamline Hotel. Florida Master Site File, file #VO9340. Florida Division of Historical Resources.

ABOUT THE AUTHOR

Robert Redd is a native Floridian with a longtime interest in history. He is a graduate of Stetson University with a degree in American studies, and he is currently pursuing his master's degree in public history. He is a member of the Florida Historical Society, the St. Augustine Historical Society, the Civil War Trust and several other historical organizations. He was previously the executive director for the New Smyrna Museum of History, and he currently works in the cultural arts field. This is Robert's fourth book with Arcadia Publishing. He lives south of the "World's Most Famous Beach" and Daytona International Speedway with his wife, Christina; dogs Finley and Ruby; and cat, Ignatius.